THE WHITE COMPANY
LONDON

THE ART OF LIVING WITH WHITE

A YEAR OF INSPIRATION

CHRISSIE RUCKER

CONTRIBUTING EDITOR & CREATIVE CONSULTANT: ALI HEATH

HARPER
DESIGN
An Imprint of HarperCollins Publishers

Contents

Introduction

— BY CHRISSIE RUCKER —

Over the last few years, our homes have become more important than ever before. As the world has changed and working more from home has become part of normal life, it also means they have had to work even harder.

While versatility and functionality are as imperative as creating a harmonious style, many of us have come to realize that it is not enough for a home to work practically or simply look stylish. It also has to feel good and bring about a sense of everyday happiness and comfort. That elusive quality is hard to pinpoint, but when it exists, it is something we are intensely aware of the moment we walk through the door. It is a feeling driven by sensory, often simple pleasures, the individuality of the owner, a warm welcome and an underlying sense of peace.

I have always loved the inherent calm that comes with living with white and neutrals, and at home this enhances the feeling of space, light and connectivity. So, in our second book, I was curious to explore how a group of inspiring, creative individuals have mastered their own way of living with white. Being invited into the worlds of these fashion designers, architects, antique dealers, property renovators, a sculptor, a fine artist and a doctor has been a privilege. Their mutual love of white comes to life in very different ways – and each owner's compelling story shines through in the design of their home.

Whether urban or rural, large or small, what makes each home truly special is not driven by its size, location or even style. It is about how everything comes together and how it feels to live in. Each home is a living entity – a unique, characterful, sensory space full of considered personal touches that bring pleasure – which evolves over time and through the seasons.

These seasonal styling ideas are inspirational and show us all how easy it can be to create fresh new looks. When accompanied by simple seasonal rituals, they help us make the most of our spaces, so we can enjoy the brightness of spring, the warmth of summer, the cosiness of autumn and the crispness of winter.

For some, the ability to nurture and style a welcoming home is an inherent part of their creative personality, while for others, including me, the process can feel much more daunting. However, I have learned over the last 27 years (from the many wonderful stylists and designers I have been lucky enough to work with) that it really is not as difficult as I first thought – and in fact today it is something I enjoy enormously.

When it comes to creating new ranges for The White Company, I am often inspired by images of a beautifully curated home. I really hope you will enjoy all the wonderful ideas these very different, enriching homes offer. They have all captured my imagination in their own unique way, and I hope they spark the seed of fresh inspiration for you too.

Chrissie x

'A passion for white unites this collection of homes,
but it is each owner's authentic creative imprint that brings
the art of living with white to life, in different ways.
With each home comes personality, warmth and that elusive
sense of comfort and calm.'

I

SPRING

Industrial Edge

— REPURPOSED SCHOOLHOUSE —

Some homes conjure a deeply emotional reaction, so appealing and unique
are their interiors, and it comes as no surprise to learn that for Lucille
Lewin creativity and storytelling sit at the heart of everything she does.
'As a sculptor I am driven by a world of imagination. The idea of creating
something out of nothing, with a strong personal narrative, has always
appealed – whether in business or at home.'

The former 19th-century Victorian schoolhouse that Lucille shares with
her husband Richard had been repurposed as a button store for London's
rag trade. The couple bought it in the 1980s and used it as an atelier for
Whistles, their pioneering fashion brand, which they had founded in 1976.
With Lucille as Creative Director, and Richard, a Harvard graduate, as the
business brains, they created a visionary new world set between fast fashion
and high-end design.

Once dilapidated and considered to be in the wrong part of town, the
now highly covetable Marylebone space has been brought back to life
with the couple's ever-evolving story. After the sale of Whistles in 2001,
the schoolhouse became a showroom for their second business, Chiltern
Street Studio, as well as a location for high-profile brand launches, events
and weddings. Lucille then worked for a short time as Creative Director
at Liberty before reconnecting with her fine art roots, graduating with a
Master's in Ceramics and Glass from the Royal College of Art in 2017.
Keen to downsize from their nearby Regency home, but determined
to avoid anything dull and ordinary, they transformed the schoolhouse
into their home.

BEST OF BOTH

In the sitting room, the traditional styles of the oversized handmade
sofas and striped ottoman, by South African Craig Kaplan, are balanced
by the pared-back design of the white chairs that Lucille found in a
Lewes junk shop. The walls are painted throughout in a combination of
Strong White by Farrow & Ball, and Cotton I by Paint & Paper Library.

An unassuming gate leads into the striking courtyard (see previous page) – more Antwerp industrial than high-street London. Bursting with dense, oversized ferns, patina-rich antique tables and chairs, and a collection of aged green urns that belonged to Lucille's mother, the enchanted space sets the tone for what is to come. 'Spring for us marks the beginning of the year: blue skies open up, birdsong returns and the earth comes alive. Surrounded by sycamore, oak and beech trees, we are in the heart of London, but the space feels mystical, protected and quiet.'

The courtyard borders an impressive run of floor-to-ceiling, sliding steel windows. Framed by imposing cast-iron pillars, the ground floor of the old schoolhouse brings together furniture and decorative finds from many different eras, pieces anchored by an instinctive 'wabi-sabi' sense of perfect imperfection and timeworn materials – think vintage hemp, ticking, battered leather, wool and soft-hued velvets. Custom-made white shelves run the length of the room, doubling as a gallery space for Lucille's crystalline, coral-like, porcelain clay sculptures, and connect to the spacious dining and kitchen area.

Designed by Lucille, in collaboration with Plain English, the metal kitchen units are a mix of freestanding-meets-fitted, offset by hardworking marble surfaces and a rustic dining table surrounded by charred comb-back Windsor chairs from HOWE. Behind the intuitive sense of calm, the high-tech heart of the house, controlled from Lucille's phone, is hidden within an over-kitchen mezzanine, along with a functional utility space.

The brief for the architects Seth Stein and Neil Wilson was to maintain the historical integrity and provenance of the schoolhouse. Throughout the building, steel girders, pillars and original tiled stairwells have been left exposed. When the ground floor collapsed during the two-year renovation, architectural salvage specialists LASSCO were called upon to source replacement salvaged floorboards. Their weathered patina in this lofty space, combined with the industrial brickwork and whitewashed walls, evokes a peaceful, ethereal elegance.

Furniture, propped art and intriguing objets take you on a personal journey, from the couple's formative roots in South Africa to their travels, work and impeccable artistic discoveries. 'For interiors to be authentic, they have to work that way. It is interesting to be at this stage, with us having lived with the space for so long and there having being so many different creative environments here – the changing alchemy is like stitching together the threads of our past, present and future,' says Lucille.

Upstairs, high-ceilinged former classrooms have been reconfigured into two bedrooms, a bathroom, a steam room and a private studio for Lucille. These are connected by a bright passageway, which is home to a quiet study area opposite a striking cabinet of curiosities from Puckhaber (shown on page 31). 'In the '60s, my mother had a beautiful interiors shop in South Africa, and sourced exquisite homeware from all over the world. It was hugely theatrical, and after school and university, I would rearrange the store and window displays – it triggered a passion for storytelling. Every piece is here because it fired my imagination or caught my eye. Things have to be loved. It is never about fashion or trends,' says Lucille.

With the exception of an armoire filled with cherished and colourful Hylton Nel pottery, the collections are saturated and muted – a ubiquitous mix of white and earthier tones. 'The space demands a respect for its heritage,' says Lucille. Compositions and displays feature Lucille's enigmatic works, alongside sculptural natural finds and treasured pieces by friends, makers and artists, including Kaori Tatebayashi.

'Growing up barefoot by the sea, amid the horrors and social upheavals of apartheid, nature was always a constant source of inspiration and calm. My sculptures are of nature and humanity, but never representational. Ideas come from a very deep place inside of me and form a narrative through time that is immensely autobiographical.'

Temporary exhibitions of Lucille's work have been curated at home, the V&A, Christie's, the contemporary craft and design fair Collect at the Saatchi Gallery and for the store Connolly, in London. But for her, the pieces displayed permanently at home act as punctuation in her work. 'They delineate a boundary between something ending and something beginning. I will never part with them, they have a special meaning in the context of my story – like concentric circles, they connect, as we do with this space.'

ARTFUL DISPLAY

Intuitive displays combine a mix of old and new. Vintage finds are juxtaposed with contemporary task lighting, modern seating and abstract art by David Champion. The 18th-century chair belonged to Lucille's grandmother and was part of a vast collection of furniture that Lucille's grandfather won in a bet at Lake Garda.

Styling Inspiration

— FROM LUCILLE & RICHARD'S HOME —

SYMMETRY & STYLE

- Lucille is often drawn to pairs of antique finds. The striking leather chairs, discovered in Lisbon, are softened with checked woollen throws from Moukie Mou.
- The lush interior echoes the tranquillity of the adjacent leafy courtyard and enhances the indoor–outdoor feel.
- Collections of vintage dolly tubs, glass vases and aged metal containers contribute to the perfectly imperfect tone, as well as being ideal for planting.
- A wooden tray adds structure to the display of treasured pieces, atop the linen ottoman. The natural cues are complemented by a textural rug from Rose Uniacke.

CREATIVE DISPLAYS

- Bespoke floating shelves provide a dedicated gallery space for an ever-changing display of work.
- Propping paintings against a wall, rather than hanging them conventionally, creates a relaxed, less formal feel.
- For Lucille, there are no rules to display. Compositions are spontaneous, in the moment and never over thought.
- Using a consistent colour palette ensures a calm, cohesive feel throughout.

ALL IN THE DETAIL

- Collected garden twigs and foraged kindling introduce a sculptural charm that references Lucille's love of nature.
- Timeless ticking-striped chairs by South African Craig Kaplan enhance the earthy monochrome palette.
- Decorative cues follow the lead set by the building: timeworn and weathered, never shiny.
- Lucille plays with proportion, offsetting the scale of the building itself with handcrafted finds above the fireplace.

SITTING COMFORTABLY
The weathered dining table, bought
at Phillips auction house, creates a
welcoming central hub for friends
and close family of all ages. The
original overhead industrial pendants
acknowledge the schoolhouse heritage.

Styling Inspiration

DECORATIVE STYLE

- An assortment of storage jars enhances the visual appeal of simple store-cupboard ingredients.
- Stacked pewter plates by Stuart Patterson introduce a decorative patina to the all-white space.
- Pinch pots, handmade by Lucille, provide sculptural interest within the functional prep area.
- Mix-and-match vintage glassware creates a sense of occasion for everyday meals.

BRIGHT SIDE

- Reflective surfaces bounce the light around and add a sophisticated edge to this dedicated drinks area.
- Hardworking marble countertops combine with deep, metal base cupboards for concealing less attractive kitchen essentials.
- The original brick walls have been whitewashed, avoiding the need for additional cupboard backs.
- A less-is-more approach ensures a sense of order and calm on the minimal floating shelves.

FINISHING TOUCHES

- A well-thought-out run of cupboards incorporating breakfast, coffee and evening drink prep areas can be exposed or hidden with sliding panels made of opaque glass.
- Displays evoke memories of people and places: a gold bowl bought in Jaipur, a tray handmade by friend Anthony Collett and a charming grey ceramic pot by Margaret Howell.
- The contemporary mixer tap by Plain English has both functional and aesthetic appeal.
- The overhead lights, made to Lucille's design from reclaimed pipes, echo the industrial lines. Used throughout, they unify the different spaces.

FAVOURITE FINDS

An antique baker's table, discovered in London's Camden Passage, adds a weathered feel to the contemporary whitewashed kitchen, while textural South African beaded bottles and an aged wooden vessel, found discarded on the road during a trip to Morocco, remind Lucille of special family holidays. Black and white jugs by Stuart Patterson, accompanied by quirky candlesticks from No.1 Lewes, bring a sculptural twist.

SHELF LIFE

Open shelves create abundant display
opportunities for Lucille's eclectic
displays of white handmade ceramics,
including favourite pieces by Astier
de Villatte, Tsé & Tsé, Postcard Teas,
Margaret Howell and Maud and Mabel.
Handcrafted serving spoons and salt
and pepper pinch pots made by Lucille
add depth and patina.

SPRING BREAKFAST

— THE ART OF OCCASION —

Spring feels like the start of a new year and a time for renewal. The welcome arrival of blue skies and green shoots, and the return of distinctive birdsong mark the start of an uplifting season.

Just as nature begins to unfurl, so we shed ourselves of cocooning layers and turn our thoughts to entertaining and leisurely weekend brunches and suppers with close family and friends.

Table decoration becomes lighter in feel, seasonal flowers and branches lift our spirits, and the fragrances we use to scent our homes become fresher and prettier. Easter and the coming together of loved ones offer the chance to celebrate traditions and create new family memories. The enjoyment of more spontaneous entertaining returns.

STYLING DETAILS

— SPRING BREAKFAST —

SIMPLICITY WITH A TWIST

- Fresh whites and pretty checks make a dramatic contrast against the dark wood table.
- A simply knotted gingham napkin is finished with an asparagus fern frond for a seasonal touch.
- Elegant juice glasses are paired with clean-lined glass candlesticks that catch the early spring light.

SET THE SCENE

- Unique touches bring a sense of occasion to simple kitchen table displays.
- Lucille's earthy salt and pepper pinch pots provide tactile, visual appeal.
- Simple pillar candlesticks are used to great effect as holders for decorative quail eggs.

PERSONAL TOUCHES

- Handmade spoons by Caroline Swift balance functionality with a desire for beautiful art forms.
- Ceramics made with integrity heighten the individual appeal of seasonal settings.

CENTRE STAGE

- Stunning Ikebana displays of spring flowers run down the centre of the table.
- Simple bowls from The White Company, doubling here as decorative seasonal vessels, can be used throughout the home.
- The mix of natural materials, such as cotton, ceramic and shell, introduces a modern rustic elegance.

MONOCHROME COHESION

The steel staircase leading up to the new mezzanine
level is dressed with natural pebble finds and
works as an impromptu log store for the adjacent
fireplace. Complementing the weathered elements
is a webbed chair bought on rue de Rivoli in Paris.

COLLECTED TREASURES

A spacious corridor connects the bedrooms while
acting as a quiet area for working and display. The
vintage metal desks were discovered at Ardingly
Antiques Fair in West Sussex and Les Puces de
Saint-Ouen market in Paris. Two Karl Blossfeldt
prints from Connolly, London, sit atop simple
industrial plinths. Layered art and collections
abound, including Lucille's mother's jewellery box
above the fireplace. Internal, graphic steel windows
allow light into the adjoining master bathroom.

LIGHT & DARK

There is an abundance of natural light throughout; at night, electric blackout blinds drop down to cocoon the rooms. Heirloom dark wood antiques and earthy paintings provide decorative appeal and textural interest in the all-white rooms.

TREASURED PIECES

Upstairs, the floors were raised to give the rooms a more intimate feel. The ticking chair, designed for Lucille by Craig Kaplan, was brought back from South Africa, along with the riempie bench. The Callimaco uplighter from Artemide and the Anglepoise wall light offset the vintage painting by Richard's mother.

A PLACE TO REST

Whitewashed walls and all-white bedding from
The White Company create a peaceful haven
in which to relax. Lucille enjoys using negative
space to enhance the feeling of serenity and
calm. Anglepoise wall lights alongside antique
side tables add a bold monochrome injection
into the pared-back room.

WALL TO WALL

The thoughtfully designed, all-white dressing
area behind the sleeping space leads into an
adjoining steam room. Lucille designed the
reclaimed pipe lighting overhead in conjunction
with a French artisanal maker.

ARTFUL CURATION

Throughout Lucille's home earthy
coloured artworks and select rustic
finds are creatively displayed with an
informal elegance. Their patina and
textural appeal complement the
timeworn floorboards and white
painted brick walls.

INDUSTRIAL TONE

The floor-to-ceiling, whitewashed
brick wall doubles as a headboard, and
is paired with inviting, softly striped
bedding by The White Company.
A vintage monastic washstand, an
heirloom inlaid chair and a collection
of pebbles add a comfortable,
weathered warmth to the stark
interior. Original BTC bedside lamps
echo the industrial tone.

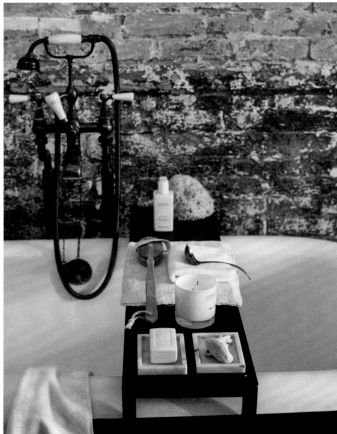

SOMETHING GOLD

Lucille always likes to introduce an element of gold
to her interiors. Never new, smart or shiny, it adds
a decadent touch to balance an industrial edge.
The gilt mirror was inherited from a neighbour
and hangs above a sink by Seth Stein, designed to
Lucille's specification. Marble soap dishes, natural
pumice and soft, white towels from The White
Company heighten the relaxed mood.

EARTHY TEXTURES

In the master bathroom, clean-lined industrial
features highlight the softer curves of the
freestanding contemporary bathtub. Carrara
marble, mixed with salvaged floorboards, lightly
washed exposed brickwork and unlacquered
Samuel Heath taps create a sophisticated elegance.
A dark wood tray is home to an heirloom silver
spoon, which Lucille uses to add Epsom salts to
her ritual evening bath.

Inside–Outside

— RURAL REINVENTION —

'When I design a building, it is important to me to preserve the original character and context – and to ensure that the new volumes created appear as if they have always belonged. Designing with care and respect is far more satisfying than adding something incongruous,' says Barbara Weiss, whose architectural ethos defines her rural Wiltshire home, which she shares with her South African husband Alan.

Barbara runs her eponymous architectural practice in Westminster, and bought this rural property nearly two decades ago as the family's out-of-London weekend escape. 'The house is set within an Area of Outstanding Natural Beauty, and we were attracted to the surrounding rolling countryside – stunning all year but particularly beautiful during the unfolding of spring. The house provided us and our three young children with a magical sense of freedom, and the opportunity to transform it into a totally bespoke home.'

Located within a quiet hamlet, tucked away at the end of a narrow lane lined with aged lime trees, the half-acre plot came complete with two Edwardian farmworker cottages dating back to 1904, which had been poorly joined together. Initially, Barbara reconfigured the plan to create a light and airy three-bedroom holiday home but, over time, as the children grew and guests multiplied, the space became too restrictive.

'Fortuitously, an opportunity arose to purchase the dilapidated cottage next door, along with a half-acre plot annexed next to ours.' The ramshackle layout, low ceilings and detachment from the main house meant it would never work as extra living space, so Barbara approached the planners with the idea of demolishing it, using the space to create a sympathetic extension that linked back to their existing home, and combining the gardens.

FIRST IMPRESSIONS

On entering the house, textural, natural materials underpin the relaxed and pared-back aesthetic. Colombe Grey stone floors from Stone Age and an inviting sheepskin chair from The White Company sit alongside a floating, Douglas fir bench, designed by Barbara. The framed pencil drawings by Agnes Martin enhance the streamlined calm.

With planning permission granted, Barbara took on the role of both client and architect, which she describes as 'immensely rewarding'. The concept for the extension was centred on achieving a strong relationship between the house and garden, with Barbara striving to create the quintessential 'inside-outside' house. New exterior vernacular brick and flint walls were built and covered in clematis, roses and hydrangeas, creating a fragrant backdrop for each season. Barbara designed a number of intricate outdoor 'rooms within rooms', each with their own proportions, levels, character and planting style, with the surrounding yew, catalpa and silver birch trees adding sculptural elegance.

'As you approach from the lane, the new two-storey extension is carefully hidden behind the original cottages, and the single-storey living area acts as a calm backdrop to herbaceous borders, which in spring are a symphony of pale greens and whites.'

Bringing the outside in and maximizing the natural light are an obsession stemming from Barbara's Italian childhood. 'Home and nature were always very connected: we lived in various flats in the heart of Milan, a mix of modern and period, linking always to the most wonderful, 16th- and 18th-century inner courtyards. Within a rather severe city, I learned to appreciate its hidden green gems and developed an interest in the relationship between architecture and design.'

A central, single-storey entrance hallway, framed by heavy steel doors and featuring a large skylight, seamlessly connects old and new. To the right are the original cottages, reconfigured to include three bedrooms, a family snug and a utility room. To the left is the new extension, with a generous open-plan kitchen-dining-living area, with large windows on three sides, and a welcoming guest suite. Upstairs are Barbara and Alan's private spaces, including a stunning en-suite master bedroom and shared study. The bright, white walls, which flow throughout, are juxtaposed with soft wood floorboards, whitewashed in a water-based emulsion to reflect the pervasive natural light.

The interior is as much about function and form as it is about the human experience. The 15-metre-long living area is cleverly zoned into well-proportioned spaces for relaxing,

eating and cooking. It comes as no surprise to learn that, with Barbara's Italian roots, entertaining is at the heart of her time in the country. The kitchen has been designed to accommodate communal cooking: 'Someone might be baking, while another is rustling up a delicious salad,' smiles Barbara. 'We run a very open house – with endless Sunday lunches and relaxed suppers for family and friends.'

Off-the-peg kitchen units, finished with bespoke, hand-painted doors, are topped with walnut and smooth Carrara marble worksurfaces. Open Douglas fir shelves – a BWA (Barbara Weiss Architects) signature design – provide storage and a display surface for Barbara's collection of white ceramics, a high–low mix of designer, high-street and artisanal pieces, discovered on trips to Paris and Capri. 'Nothing is precious, and I am always drawn to pieces of varying shape and design.'

Storage and joinery are noteworthy throughout – in fact, Barbara has written a book on the subject – and every nook optimizes her clever use of space. The elegant white interior allows Barbara's timeless furniture to take centre stage. Favourite pieces include a Hans Wegner coffee table sourced from a Chicago auction house, Galvanitas S16 Dutch School chairs, and dark red leather and chrome chairs – a 1930s design by Giuseppe Terragni.

Covetable task lighting features prominently: think Bestlite, Anglepoise and a prized Pierre Guariche sideboard lamp in the upstairs study, paired with facing Alvar Aalto desks and treasured framed prints by Bauhaus designer Anni Albers.

The bedrooms and bathrooms are relaxed affairs, tall and spacious with skylights everywhere. Beds are dressed in a mix of soft linens and crisp cottons, with furniture kept to a minimum – save for a few heirloom chairs, including a timeworn rocker and a Lloyd Loom original.

'Lying in bed, we watch the stars through the skylight, and on warm spring mornings – with the roof terrace doors flung open – we revel in the rising sun, fresh air and stillness. Apart from birds and hooting owls, the silence marks a significant shift from the bustle of London. We have nurtured a slower, easier, more natural side to our lives here. Whenever I leave, I cannot wait to get back.'

PITCH PERFECT

The pitched roofline of the new extension
is a respectful nod to the prevailing
architectural style. Seating areas have been
cleverly positioned to make the most of
the sunshine at different times of the day
and year. The more formal raised terrace
is a favourite entertaining spot, with views
across the distant rolling countryside.

COME TOGETHER

In the main living area, crisp white walls, whitewashed softwood floorboards and floaty linen curtain panels create the perfect quiet backdrop for a mix of bold mid-century-meets-new furniture and vintage lighting. Each carefully zoned area also connects independently to the surrounding garden views and terraces.

GLASS HOUSE

The black silhouette of the Westfire wood burner, which echoes the lines of the graphic steel doors, and the 1930s chrome and leather chairs by Giuseppe Terragni create drama against the bright white walls and floors. Simple white linen curtains enhance the seamless connection to the exterior.

SOFT CURVES

The round Hans Wegner coffee table punctuates the clean-lined architecture and furniture, adding a relaxed softness to the space, which is reinforced by the tactile, handcrafted white ceramics. The grey wool Linie Design rug heightens the sense of textural comfort underfoot and anchors the seating area in the open-plan design.

MIXING OLD & NEW

During the day, the long skylight and glass door wash the central dining
area in natural light, while at night, the table is punctuated by pools
of warm light from the replica Alvar Aalto hanging pendants. Barbara
designed the dining table using original Le Corbusier table legs, from
twentytwentyone, and a custom-made, three-metre-long Douglas
fir top, and surrounded it with Galvanitas S16 Dutch school chairs.
Artisanal Portuguese ceramics and napkins from The White Company
offset the woody tones.

BEST DRESSED

Entertaining is at the core of this home, so a generous supply of simple
white crockery and glassware is a prerequisite. The Douglas fir open
shelves, designed by BWA (Barbara Weiss Architects), add personality
and warmth to the kitchen, while providing practical storage, to create
a space that feels lived in, loved and welcoming.

MIX & MATCH

The modern kitchen, with its contemporary Concetto tap
from hansgrohe, two ovens and two sinks, combines function
with form. Custom-made cabinet doors, Carrara marble and
walnut worksurfaces, as well as high-end hardware, embellish
the off-the-peg cabinet carcasses. Wooden chopping boards
from The White Company and leafy plants underline the
connection with nature.

HOME STUDY

A pair of facing classic Artek desks, by Alvar Aalto, are balanced by a wall-mounted, 1920s Danish sideboard in the upstairs study. The artworks, sourced by Alan, include a collection of framed prints by Anni Albers, 1920s Russian constructivism drawings and more colourful architectural prints by Aldo Rossi, complementing the white interior.

THINK BESPOKE

In the master bedroom, with its roof terrace, the striking
oversized headboard is a simple piece of oak-veneered
MDF. The wall-mounted 1960s bedside tables, which were
found online, follow the floating joinery theme that prevails
throughout. Adding to the calm, natural feel is the layered
linen bedding from The White Company.

NATURAL SELECTION

Bathrooms are left clutter-free, and natural materials
take the lead. In the master bathroom, a striking
walnut vanity, topped by richly veined Carrara
marble, is home to stacks of soft white towels from
The White Company. Sculptural greenery connects
to the landscape beyond.

Styling Inspiration

— FROM BARBARA'S HOME —

PRACTICALITIES & WELLBEING

- In a home where there is a love of entertaining, peaceful guest rooms, providing both comfort and functionality, are a priority.
- Layers of inviting bed linen and textural throws add sensory enjoyment, while practical task lighting is positioned at the right height for bedtime reading.
- Considering lighting and the position of fixings at the start of a project prevents expensive mistakes.
- A pretty water glass and decanter are a personal touch that makes guests feel at home.

CREATIVE CORNERS

- Barbara always works with the nuances of a space to create bespoke storage and joinery solutions, ensuring that each room has its own character and purpose.
- With its small window, a quiet nook in a guest bedroom has been artfully transformed into a minuscule but charming desk and dressing table.
- A wall-to-wall piece of whitewashed wood creates an affordable desk.
- Softening the overall look and adding decorative charm is a comfy vintage chair.

LET THERE BE LIGHT

- Light is of paramount importance to Barbara. Each window in the home frames a specific view, whether a detail in the garden, or the fields beyond.
- Simple white roller blinds keep window treatments to a bare minimum, allowing natural light to flood in unrestricted during the day.
- Barbara has painted walls, ceilings and woodwork in just one shade, Dulux Brilliant White, which maximizes the light levels and avoids harsh contrast lines.

NOSTALGIC BLUES

Despite Barbara's children now being in their late twenties and mid-thirties, their childhood bedroom, with four single beds, in the original cottage has been preserved intact for new generations of young visitors. Smart pale blue panelling doubles as a headboard, while clever underbed storage ensures a clutter-free space.

SPRING HOME RITUALS

I love it when the seasons change, as it marks the beginning of a new and exciting phase. Keeping our homes in order and at their best is an ongoing commitment, but this is what makes them so special and ensures they continue to evolve over time. After a long winter, the arrival of spring always feels so welcome, and it is the perfect season to refresh our homes. These are some of the rituals I like to do at this time of year, which help to set us up for the warmer months ahead.

Book in maintenance and decorating jobs. Spring and summer are the perfect time for these, and it's amazing what a difference repairing a broken handle or applying a fresh coat of paint can make.

•

Clean, declutter and reorganize cupboards and shelves. Bring forward key spring and summer pieces and push back casserole dishes and winter clothes. It's a good time now to sell or give away pieces we no longer use. Having space, a place for everything and the pieces we love easily to hand, creates a wonderful sense of calm and order.

•

Pack away wintry sheepskins, faux fur throws and cushions. Store them in breathable cotton bags until you are ready to bring them out again in the autumn. Replace them with fresh cottons, cool linens and soft layers of tactile wool or cashmere.

•

Give your bed a spring lift with lighter layers and a fresher look. Turn your mattress (every three months is ideal) and launder pillows, duvets and mattress covers. Pack away 13.5-tog duvets and switch to a 9-tog or lower. Check the age of your pillows – if you sleep on them every night, they should ideally be renewed every two to three years, to give proper support and prevent allergies.

Launder curtains and have carpets and furniture professionally cleaned, if necessary. Shake out rugs and hang them outside to air on a sunny day.

•

Finish or pack away Christmassy home scents and bath treats. Repurpose their glass holders as tealight holders, glasses or vases. Change the scent of candles, diffusers and room sprays for the new season. Some of my favourite notes for spring include everything from cut grass, rose and honeysuckle to geranium, tuberose and cashmere woods.

•

Give glass vases a refresh. Soaking them with a denture cleaning tablet helps to remove water marks and get them sparkling again. Switch up your flower and foliage choices – even just a few simple sprigs will lift a table or room. My favourites include parrot tulips and anemones, year-round herbs such as rosemary, and pretty varieties of eucalyptus and wild cow parsley. Potted bulbs, hyacinths or narcissi are wonderful too, as are budding cherry tree branches, which will begin to bloom when they come indoors.

•

Power-hose outdoor stone terraces and garden furniture, ready for the first warm spring days.

•

Start to pot white summer plants – pelargoniums are wonderful indoors and out.

II

SUMMER

Heart & Soul

The Hampshire property that Tim Evans shares with his two children captures the essence of what makes a home special. Built out of passion and tenacity, it weaves a story of love, loss and hope. In the rich tapestry of life, tragedy often takes hold when we least expect it, and at those times, home, family and friends become the foundations that get us through.

Tim sadly lost his wife Annabel in 2008 after she was diagnosed with cancer five years earlier, when their children, Wilf and Poppy, were aged just two and one. Annabel had carved out a successful interior design career, working collaboratively with Veere Grenney and Colefax and Fowler, and had a well-respected creative eye. Throughout her surgery and treatment, she continued working on the renovation of numerous houses for her family, which kept her spirits up. Each sale – seven, over eight years of marriage – took them further up the property ladder, culminating with Annabel's final project and the fulfilment of a personal dream, to build this country home.

'Before meeting Annabel, I had enjoyed doing a few solo renovation projects, so was used to working with architects and garden designers,' says Tim. 'When we were introduced, I was attracted to Annabel's passion for design. She had great energy, humour and intellect, and, at six-feet tall, with bold opinions on life, she stood out. Her personality and unique, eclectic fashion sense drew people in, and within each of our homes, her individual style was felt.'

The stunning brick and flint house sits at the end of a bumpy, quarter-mile track, surrounded by pleached plane trees and lavender. 'You know you are in the country when you leave tarmac behind and feel your shoulders

LOVE WHAT YOU FIND

Annabel believed in sourcing only what you truly love, such as these bricks from Belgium and roof tiles from Spain. The attractive slate roof of the porch sets an immediately welcoming tone as you walk up to the house. Wisteria and white climbing roses frame the porch, and their fragrant tones are carried through into the house, with its vases of cut flowers and scented candles.

drop,' says Tim. On arrival, you are greeted by the children's guinea fowl – the last ones standing after being incubated and hatched as part of a school project – and two rough-coated lurchers, Monty and Willa, who treat the guinea fowl as part of the pack. 'Annabel had always wanted dogs here – their arrival completed the final piece of the puzzle.'

With the exception of the dogs, every other imaginable detail had been taken care of, and the plot was transformed from a muddy dig to an extraordinary country home in just nine months. With 360-degree views across open farmland, the Georgian-style house feels immediately warm and welcoming, with the imposing volumes of room heights, doorways and windows softened by personal, tactile layers.

Following Wilf's birth, the family rented a former farm labourer's cottage on the land, as a weekend escape. When the owner decided to sell, they were given first refusal and worked with trusted local architect Barry Bowhill to transform the plot into a permanent home. A week before completion, the old cottage was razed to the ground, and landscaper Nick Tripp planted the garden, to Annabel's design, with climbing wisteria, clematis, jasmine, rambling roses, alliums, Annabelle hydrangeas, yew hedges and a mix of formal and informal spaces, including the inviting pool house. 'In the summer, when the children return from university with all their friends, the house becomes very sociable – with pool barbecues, long lunches and, for Wilf, some form of cricket on the lawn,' smiles Tim.

The decorative front porch sits centrally on the double-fronted façade, framed with lofty bay windows and shuttered sashes. Expectations of a traditional Georgian layout quickly give way to a space that is more New England in feel, with the front hall rising up to pitch-perfect vaulted elevations on the top landing and throughout the elegant bedrooms and bathrooms. 'When the ceilings started to go in upstairs, it felt as if we were losing something unique, so we took them down and integrated the roofline as a feature.'

These striking gestures are matched downstairs with thoughtful, more symmetrical spaces that make the most of the layout. The walls are lined with horizontal wood cladding and fabric wallpapers in calming palettes, enhancing the well-chosen antiques, rugs, collections of objets and pieces of art. The rooms and hallways are filled with impromptu seating, dressed in vintage linens and all manner of beautiful textiles. The library sofa – Tim's favourite – is upholstered in a Veere Grenney fabric, designed by Annabel (see page 86).

The library is also home to a treasured partners desk, which the couple bought together. Tim has filled the bookcase with travel, interior design and medical books, which reference his medical background and role as Apothecary to HM the Queen and The Royal Households of London.

At the heart of the house, the kitchen opens up into a light, bright space, which looks out over peaceful English countryside, where the quiet is occasionally interrupted by the sound of a distant train. 'We are very exposed to the elements, but in summer, doors are flung open, the surrounding fields come alive with colourful seed and wheat, and a wonderful breeze filters through the house. It is a beautiful season here,' says Tim.

The kitchen, a traditional handmade Plain English design, is juxtaposed with decorative antiques – a beautiful blue-grey, heavily patinated dresser from Josephine Ryan, and stunning antique French shelves displaying a collection of beautiful glassware. 'Poppy has inherited her mum's culinary skills and is always experimenting, which is a real treat,' says Tim.

'We have been connected to this land since the children were babies – both learned to walk, talk and ride their bikes here, and I have been blessed to enjoy many happy celebrations with them. I think Annabel knew this would be her last project, and when she left for the last time, she had thought of every detail, leaving no instructions, simply trusting us to make it our home.'

Beneath the beautiful veneer, this family home is so much more than the sum of its parts. With a relaxed sense of comfort and happiness, it is imbued with a quiet, inspirational legacy that will never be forgotten.

HALLWAY HUB

Off-white reclaimed marble floor tiles add a
soulful patina to the back hallway, home to
a family piano and large comfy sofas, which
create welcoming reasons to linger and enjoy
this generous space. The central antique table,
sideboard and patina-rich enamel light were
sourced by Annabel from Ardingly Antiques
Fair in West Sussex, England.

Styling Inspiration

VOLUME & LIGHT

- Instead of adding ceiling boards, as originally intended, the internal roofline has been left exposed to make the most of the space.
- Horizontal cladding painted white gives a New England flavour and complements the lofty feel, along with the 8-foot-high doorways.
- Custom-made bookcases and the vintage chests of drawers create a welcoming, lived-in feel.
- A vintage floor runner and patterned wallpaper have gentle, textural appeal, while a series of white pendant lights adds a more contemporary air.

UP CLOSE & PERSONAL

- Treasured collections, including carved animals bought from a street seller during a family holiday to Zimbabwe, are displayed on an antique sideboard.
- The beautiful bronze cast of Annabel was made when the children were tiny, and her presence is a vital part of what makes this space feel like home.
- Vintage botanical prints discovered by the couple are a nod to a shared love of gardens and horticulture.
- Branches are frequently cut from the garden and add sculptural appeal to the interior.

ALL ABOUT TEXTURE

- An antique sofa reupholstered in vintage linen creates comfortable seating in the back hallway.
- Low-hung artwork draws the eye in, its palette complementing the tones found in the cladding, floors and textiles.
- A patina-rich wall lantern adds a soft glow to the basement stairs at night.

DEFINING FEATURES

The use of white in the Plain English kitchen – for the
cabinetry and marble, as well as the tableware, chairs,
lighting and flowers – creates a unifying elegance.
The varying shades, textures and patinas provide
a rich layered canvas as the backdrop to convivial
family lunches and day-to-day life.

NATURAL PATINA

Everyday items displayed in vintage containers, stacked
casually in an old armoire or grouped on open hanging
rails, ensure the kitchen displays are both functional and
aesthetically pleasing. The old railway clock, discovered
by Annabel at the Maison&Objet trade show in Paris, is
paired with a beautiful antique table.

ALL ABOUT THE LIGHT

During his early career, Tim spent time in
Zimbabwe as the District Medical Officer
of a remote hospital on the shores of
Lake Kariba. The extraordinary sense of
light and space that he experienced there
influenced how he wanted to live back in
the UK. Annabel worked this inspiration
into their home, creating curtain-free
window vistas in every room.

SUMMER BRUNCH

— THE ART OF OCCASION —

With the delight of long days, warm sunshine and spectacular sunsets, summer is when many of us are at our most sociable.

Our homes come alive with children, extended family and visiting friends. With fresh ingredients at their best, meals become occasions to be savoured. Relaxed kitchen lunches, poolside barbecues and coastal picnics foster a feeling of togetherness.

Tables can be dressed effortlessly but to great effect with just a few simple sprigs, whether from the local flower stall or the garden, and some airy linens.

STYLING DETAILS

— S U M M E R   B R U N C H —

FINISHING DETAILS

- Thoughtfully dressed tables create a warm welcome.
- Low-level fluted glassware gives a relaxed yet immensely elegant feel.
- Textured bobble jugs for water and fresh homemade lemonade have decorative appeal.
- Small glass bud vases ensure flower displays do not encroach on conversations across the table.

WHITE ON WHITE

- A palette of all-white table accessories adds to the summery feel.
- Various shades and textures of white have a layered, tactile appeal.
- Fabric placemats and simply folded napkins are part of the welcoming, laid-back vibe.
- Decorative white bobble plates and sparkling glassware bring a sense of occasion to a simple lunch.

SEASONAL STYLE

- Bring the outside in to create displays that are personal to the home.
- Natural garden finds in tabletop displays effortlessly connect with the verdant seasonal story outside.
- Single-stem flowers and wild grasses bring a timeless and calm quality to the relaxed country look.
- A patina-rich, scrubbed antique table adds a rustic feel to the comfortable kitchen setting.

DECORATIVE DISPLAY

- Simple open shelves showcase a personal narrative.
- In the kitchen-dining area, the antique cupboard makes a wonderful nook for collections of glassware.
- The charming antique table is the perfect alternative to a drinks trolley, with glasses presented on a silver tray.
- Tapered white candles and a jug of flowers decorate the table beautifully.

DECORATIVE DETAILS

Bespoke wooden shutters avoid the need
for heavy curtains, while optimizing the
natural light. A vast antique cupboard
hides less attractive media equipment
and provides valuable storage for albums,
photos and books. Sofas, lampshades
and cushions have been designed with
favourite fabrics and incorporate a variety
of textures and patterns.

A RELAXED DISPOSITION

Looking out onto the garden, this inviting
spot by the French doors is the epitome
of comfort, with a favourite antique chair,
covered in a soft, pale pink-patterned fabric
that sits perfectly with the vintage hemp
on the upholstered circular ottoman.
Textural details abound, and a pretty side
table plays host to a collection of framed
family photos.

BY MY SIDE

Tim likes to sit at his desk with a fire in the grate, and the dogs either at his feet or curled up on the armchairs. Thoughtfully curated art and books fill the library with personality. Natural textures – the sisal carpet, rustic overhead pendant, dry-scraped armoire and tactile vintage linens – accentuate the welcoming tone.

CANOPY OF DREAMS

A fabric-covered canopy designed by
Annabel adds impact to the master
bedroom as it enjoys the first rays of
morning sunshine. Fresh, white bedding
from The White Company and a wonderful
bedspread lend textural appeal, while
the photographs, art and sculptures of the
children when they were young make
the space truly personal.

CALM ESCAPE

A collection of decorative pill boxes and scent bottles gives an eclectic edge to a simple antique dressing table in the master bedroom. A white lace cloth and sculptural white flowers add a feminine touch, offset by a gently patterned wallpaper.

SITTING PRETTY

Taking centre stage in the vaulted master en-suite is an antique bathtub from Drummonds, London. The corner shower, which is cleverly boxed-in and concealed, has breathtaking views across the open countryside. Layers of inviting soft towels from The White Company are stacked on a decorative footstool, while art and natural finds add a personal touch.

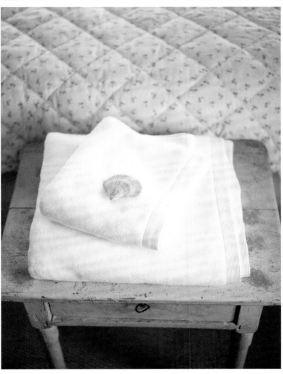

TWIN SET

Annabel sourced beautiful matching antique beds for both her daughter's and son's bedrooms, creating the most magical sleeping spaces for them and their friends to enjoy. In Poppy's room, the softest pink bed throws, gingham cushions and table lamp add a feminine touch to the all-white scheme.

SOFT DETAILS

In the children's bathroom, double sinks are paired with clever hidden storage above, and a comfy armchair for enjoying the country view. A decorative pink shell acts as a reminder of a fun family holiday, while in Poppy's bedroom, simple white and glass vases from The White Company provide the opportunity for cheerful floral displays.

WHITE & BRIGHT

The airy, whitewashed pool house forms a pleasing
backdrop to the inviting pool and elegant white
sunloungers. Glazed doors open to a dining table
surrounded by French Tolix chairs and a comfy bench
seat layered with plump cushions.

Styling Inspiration

LAYER UP

- Layered with a mix of linen pillows and quilted cotton cushions from The White Company, the swinging daybed encourages you to kick back and relax.
- Using indoor bedding as a solution for summer outdoor seating means that purchases work hard for all seasons.
- A frilled linen sheet from The White Company doubles up as an outdoor cover.
- The floaty layers evoke a nostalgic feeling of carefree holidays, to be savoured and enjoyed.

REST & RETREAT

- The pool house is the perfect spot for cooling off in the shade and enjoying a light lunch. Simple earthenware plates, linen napkins and rustic placemats from The White Company create a relaxed, informal feel.
- Garden cuttings in a vintage jug enhance the relaxed country vibe and mirror the flower borders.
- Simple metal Tolix chairs contribute a French holiday feel, and their weathered patina ensures a relaxed pool-house atmosphere.

TIME TO REFLECT

- Blousy Annabelle hydrangeas complement the decorative white layers on the handcrafted swinging daybed by Sitting Spiritually, which Tim discovered at The Chelsea Flower Show.
- The weathered frame is perfect in all conditions. In summer, it comes alive with textural cushions and covers.
- Climbing plants add a fragrant canopy to the seating frame, positioned under an oak tree planted in memory of Annabel.

Sartorial Elegance

For couturier Anna Valentine, there is an overwhelming similarity between the principles behind her atelier and the way she has designed her London apartment. Yet it is the sense of atmosphere at the core of this home's refined DNA that leaves the strongest imprint. It is a graceful space, without pretence, where less is definitely more.

'When I relocated my atelier to a nearby Marylebone mews in 2011, we fell in love with the area and decided to move from our Victorian house in Shepherd's Bush,' says Anna. The impeccable, first-floor Georgian apartment, which Anna shares with husband Jonathan Berger, who works in the film and TV industry, had been untouched for 30 years: 'Despite the yellow Formica kitchen, boxy dark rooms and low false ceilings, we were immediately drawn to the potential, proportions and location.'

The kitchen overlooks a private garden square, full of plane trees, and in summer the neighbourhood comes alive with the sounds of schoolchildren playing, dogs barking, birdsong and local church bells. 'Home is just a short stroll to the studio – it is central, but enjoys a village-like feel. Every morning Jonathan and I ritually walk our lurchers, Ghengis and Saffy, in the surrounding parks before collecting coffee and beginning our workdays.'

Anna's love of fashion began at a young age, making clothes for her dolls while following her passion for ballet. 'My mother is incredibly creative and encouraged me to sew and make – I was the original *Blue Peter* child,' laughs Anna, who in her early twenties turned her childhood hobby into a sideline that paid for her expensive dance classes. When the door to a career in dance closed at the age of 23, fashion took centre stage.

HIGH–LOW

The setting of this low-level, minimal kitchen in a soaring space with oversized original windows creates a tension that is both inspiring and grounding. Touches of bold black bring contrast and definition to the all-white interior, while sculptural branches add a seamless connection to the leafy square opposite.

Anna channelled her energy, learning on the job and spending hours perfecting her technique, before setting up her own eponymous couture and ready-to-wear label. Working with a team of in-house designers, pattern cutters, fitters and seamstresses, she has achieved prodigious success over the past three decades, most famously designing the Duchess of Cornwall's celebrated wedding outfit. Discerning clients are drawn to Anna's perfectly tailored, timeless classics, which combine contemporary raw edges, exquisite hand-finished embellishment and bespoke natural fabrics, such as her trademark Double Duchess Satin, dyed by artisan specialists to Anna's exacting palette, with a patina akin to soft Italian plasterwork. 'Having trained as a ballet dancer, it made me very aware of proportion, movement and how things fall on the body. Working personally with my clients and perfecting a design for them is very special, as it is about making a person feel the best they can.'

Understated, flattering and designed with huge attention to detail, Anna's creations have the illusion of effortless simplicity, and this translates into how she has decorated her home. Throughout the apartment, elegant architectural bones and natural materials are given space to breathe, accentuated by furniture and collections that read as textures – unfussy, relaxed and inviting, yet inherently sophisticated. 'We have visited Japan a few times and their wabi-sabi philosophy and view of architecture appeal to us both.'

With that in mind, the couple commissioned DRDH Architects to help restore the property. 'They presented paintings from the 19th-century home of Danish artist Vilhelm Hammershøi, at Strandgade 30. His interiors resonated with the calm, sparse style we were keen to achieve, paired with restful interior tones and the artistic use of scale on diverse door and window heights.'

Partition walls were removed and spaces reconfigured, to allow the natural light to flow freely through from the original, floor-to-ceiling glazed doors at the front of the apartment to the master bedroom balcony at the back. The entire two-bedroom space is united by custom-made shuttered windows, reclaimed parquet floors and intricate cornicing, commissioned from a tiny, on-site fragment of original plasterwork.

The kitchen itself has an ethereal feel, with custom-made cabinetry and utilitarian marble surfaces that are echoed through similarly stark bathrooms. To balance the minimal aesthetic, an oversized cupboard conceals kitchen appliances and the more unsightly essentials of daily life. The theme continues with linking hallway cabinets, and a master bedroom divide that anchors thoughtfully hidden storage, with a defining architectural view – a gentle nod to Hammershøi's own spaces.

The tall minimally decorated walls are painted in Farrow & Ball's Strong White and conceal a projector and a state-of-the-art speaker system. 'The negative white space encourages a wonderful interplay of light and shadow, which is very calming,' says Anna, who always considers every single detail. 'I move things around until they feel just so; and it is the same with cushions, textiles and natural finds. They have to look right – squashed and lived-in, never formal. I prefer simple leaves to flowers, and am always searching for fallen branches with beautiful shape and form.'

Furniture follows similar sculptural lines: a bespoke sofa from Studio Oliver Gustav and a dining table from Vincent Van Duysen, surrounded by antique chairs discovered in Fayence in France, as well as weathered artisanal Chinese stools from 1819 Antiques, one of the couple's favourite antique haunts.

'I like to display more humble collections of white and earthy-hued antique ceramics, in decorative clusters, alongside more precious pieces by Paul Philippe, Akiko Hirai, Lucie Rie, Edmund de Waal and early degree-show sculptures by friend Lucille Lewin (see page 10). I often find inspiring household pieces in UK store Freight. Usuhari glassware, handblown in Tokyo, by Shotoku, is also a favourite.'

Throughout, scent is presented as an occasion to be enjoyed: Japanese oils on wood blocks in wardrobes and Pot Pourri Apothicaire lava rocks in the sitting room. 'I don't like scents to overwhelm, so use them occasionally, as I do perfume. With restraint, an atmosphere can be savoured and enjoyed, like the preparation of Friday evening drinks or Jonathan's homemade sushi.'

'Our home feeds my soul,' says Anna. 'It is our sanctuary and we feel blessed to live here. For us it is the perfect fit.'

SPACE TO BREATHE

The minimalist kitchen is offset by the
weathered texture of the stools and the wooden
floorboards. The powder-coated wall lights
from Skinflint and a reclaimed floor lamp from
Retrouvius give a soft focus with their curved
edges and warm light.

Styling Inspiration

— FROM ANNA & JONATHAN'S HOME —

ALL IS CALM

- The oversized kitchen cupboard cleverly conceals the fridge, freezer and all manner of kitchen store-cupboard essentials, creating a sense of order and tranquillity.
- The white wooden doors complement the relaxed Farrow & Ball Strong White walls throughout the home.
- Displays of treasured ceramic collections bring a textural earthiness to the pared-back interior.
- Organic materials – marble, wood, ceramic and stone – add to the sense of composure and serenity.

SET IN STONE

- The striking marble backsplash has been inset into the wall for a smooth, flush finish.
- Stacks of patina-rich stone bowls create a textural still life on the clean marble surface.
- Vintage French and Italian confit pots provide unique storage for vintage spoons, rolling pins and ladles.
- Simple black and white ceramic oil bottles add a contemporary modern edge as well as reflecting the couple's love of cooking.

EVERYDAY RITUALS

- The Japanese tea set is a favourite from Maud and Mabel, London.
- The calming ceremony of making tea and creating a sense of occasion with beautiful ceramics is important to Anna.
- Touches of black within the all-white space add contrast and depth, along with fresh pops of green, a nod to the garden square opposite.
- The placement of a simple reading lamp directs low-level light and avoids harsh overhead sources – a practice enjoyed in every room.

WEATHERED & WORN
A tribal antique stool from Peter Adler, London, topped with a decorative off-cut of marble stands next to a rattan armchair, sourced from 1819 Antiques, which complements the elegant, custom-made sofa from Studio Oliver Gustav.

ALL WHITE

The master bedroom is layered in textural bedding
from The White Company. Floor-to-ceiling shelves
on one side of the bed offer valuable storage for books
and magazines while creating a welcoming, lived-in
feel. Jonathan planned out the run of intuitively
designed storage that divides the bedroom from
the linking hallway.

LINE OF SIGHT

The table in front of the balcony window of the master
bedroom enjoys a view through the length of the apartment
and out across neighbouring rooftops. Made from an old cruise
liner support, it was sourced from Stephen Sprake Antiques
in London. An antique bentwood chair complements the
collection of artworks by Antoni Tàpies.

Styling Inspiration

— FROM ANNA & JONATHAN'S HOME —

SYNERGY & REPETITION

- Anna enjoys the repetition of surfaces throughout the apartment. The bathroom panelling and sink stand echo the Carrara marble used in the kitchen.
- The all-white bathroom scheme features a collection of vintage earthenware. Displayed close together, the pots increase their textural impact.
- A false ceiling in the bathroom provides additional storage space, helping to keep the main living area free of clutter.
- The large mirror optimizes the light and sense of space.

MOODY HUES

- Dark, earthy vessels from South Africa make attractive storage for bath salts, natural stones, pumice and artisanal soap, while creating contrast within the white apartment.
- Adding to the wabi-sabi joy of perfect imperfection, the rustic stool contributes to the overall feeling of warmth.
- The juxtaposition of battered surfaces with smooth marble finishes heightens the understated sense of chic.
- Making time for ritual baths creates a sanctuary-style calm that relaxes and rejuvenates.

NEW HEIGHTS

- The high-ceilinged wet room with its marble floor reiterates the ethereal elegance of the generously proportioned apartment.
- Textural Portuguese wall tiles of varying lengths impart an air of simplicity as well as sophistication.
- The contemporary look of the sleek Vola taps and stone sink are offset by the wooden stool and sculptural branch, which give a natural ambience to the space.

HARDWORKING SPACES

Anna's at-home studio is easily transformed
into a sleeping area with the elegant daybed
from The Conran Shop. The vintage wooden
stools from Clignancourt flea market in Paris,
the chest of drawers and the herringbone
flooring, along with Anna's collections of
notebooks, vintage spools, scissors, pebbles
and storage baskets, impart a very lovely
softness to the white space.

SUMMER HOME RITUALS

There is nothing more magical than the moment when we can throw
open the doors and begin to eat outside again. As the sun shines
and everything begins to grow, it's time to make the most of longer days,
alfresco eating, picnics and sunsets. Summer is made for entertaining
and for good times with family and friends. When the temperature rises,
these are a few of my favourite summer rituals.

Prepare for long-awaited outdoor living by
dusting off picnic baskets, non-breakable glasses
and plates, comfy outdoor cushions, seating and
picnic blankets.

•

Rediscover joyful bunting, summery table
linens, pretty cushions and soft outdoor throws,
as well as outdoor fairy lights, candle lanterns
and bistro bulbs.

•

Rearrange furniture to create space around
doorways to the garden, and throw open
windows and balcony doors. Declutter
coffee tables, stools and bedside tables for
a fresher, summery vibe.

•

Encourage a sense of indoor–outdoor living
by introducing simple movable seating, such as
sisal pouffes and stools, which work equally well
indoors or out.

•

In the kitchen, bring forward pieces that are great for
entertaining, such as big platters, large sharing boards,
summer napkins and placemats, as well as hurricane
lamps that won't blow out in a breeze.

Think about how best to serve drinks outside. A small
table or attractive, movable bar trolley, filled with
robust glassware and a large, ice-filled bottle trug,
is always a great idea.

•

During summer, my favourite flowers include white
peonies, alliums and stocks, through to white
hydrangeas, roses and sweet peas. Summer grasses
are also wonderful for the table, along with garden
mint – I always grow extra – and white lavender.

•

For candles and home scents, I love ozonic, citrus and
herbal, everything from sea salt, vetiver, rosemary
and bergamot, to neroli, lime blossom, eucalyptus
and lemongrass.

•

The optimal temperature for sleeping well is 18°C,
so keeping cool on warm summer nights can become
a challenge. It really helps to change to a lightweight,
4.5-tog duvet or just a top sheet, accompanied by
a cotton blanket or bedspread.

•

This is also the perfect time to switch to cool summer
towelling: think soft cotton waffle towels and lighter-
weight robes in micro-waffles or pure linen.

III
AUTUMN

Slow Architecture

— URBAN SANCTUARY —

For many architects, a building's form and structure are often favoured over and above ideas about contents and display. For architect Spencer Fung and his wife, designer and creative consultant Teresa Roviras, the two are inextricably linked. 'We share an unequivocal passion for nature, which sits at the heart of all,' says Spencer.

Growing up in urban Hong Kong, Spencer had a strong desire to connect with nature, which he sought out at every opportunity, and it influenced his decision to study architecture, both at Cambridge and at the Architectural Association in London. Understated and humble, he is the quiet architectural force behind many esteemed clients, loyal to his sustainable approach. By contrast, Teresa was raised in Catalonia, surrounded by the rugged vastness of the Pyrenees and the calm Mediterranean waters of Barcelona. Working as a 'visual interpreter', book designer and shopkeeper, with her own online store, Hedgehog, she too is driven by an association with the natural world. Together, their style fuses urban and rural ideals.

The couple moved to their north London, double-fronted Victorian home in 2006, when Teresa was pregnant with their second child. 'We were attracted to the scale, proportions and light, and it had a wonderful family feel,' says Teresa. The house is close to their former maisonette and surrounded by green spaces, including Hampstead Heath where the couple have fostered a love of wild swimming.

'At home everything begins with the shell,' says Spencer. Thoughtfully sourced dark grey antique marble is used for the floors, kitchen island, worktops and bathrooms, anchoring spaces with a warm, monolithic elegance, and a sense of longevity and heritage. 'Marble is an investment,

CENTRE STAGE

The whitewashed oak dining table by Spencer Fung is
surrounded by a selection of antique and heirloom dining
chairs, united by smart black linen upholstery. The original
cast-iron fireplace was stolen from the site during the
renovation and has been replaced with a reclaimed marble
design from The Architectural Forum.

but is both practical and noble,' says Spencer. 'Noble materials are a celebration of the natural, restrained and rustic, but I like to use them in fresh contemporary ways. Taking the time to find the perfect materials is important to me, as from this start point everything else flows. I am drawn to surfaces that show the marks of their past and present, and I always choose enduring stone that can be repurposed in the future.'

Set out over three levels, the house is entered via a wide hallway, with a staircase to one side. On the left, the living room looks out to the front garden, and at the back, the dining room and kitchen link to the rear garden. Attracted to the intimacy of the Victorian footprint, Spencer made the decision to work with the architecture of the original run-down building, to retain its integrity, changing only the connection of the kitchen and dining areas via a new marble-framed archway, and adding a new studio that links to the back of the house.

On the first floor, a study provides a versatile creative space, along with a restful master suite. On the top floor, the two children's rooms, a shower and a guest room follow the same sensory, visual narrative. 'The Victorians knew how to create well-proportioned spaces and, as our family has grown, the mix of both connected and separate spaces has been important.'

The bold, natural interior is enhanced by exacting attention to detail. 'Bespoke finishes are important to me, and I choose always to work with skilled artisans and local trades. It is my way of connecting to a place and its history, and the preservation of this knowledge is precious,' says Spencer. The off-white limestone plaster walls are alive with unique imperfections that show the hand of the plasterer – Spencer defines it as 'Slow Architecture'. The natural formula, developed by the architect, is hand-trowelled and its gestural, tactile finish makes it immensely characterful.

Throughout the house, collections of natural objects – dried seed heads, coral, pine cones, antlers, driftwood, bleached pebbles, worn stones, twigs and simple dried hydrangea heads – are artfully displayed as reminders of the couple's personal journey and travels. The same is true of their collections of antique curiosities, where the minimalist-palette-meets-maximalist-display unfolds behind glass display cabinets in the dining room – think stacks of covetable white and natural vintage plates, bowls and platters, curated alongside pewter dishes, stoneware jugs and vintage teapots.

Soft whites are layered with soft blacks and warm chocolate browns, all rich in texture: relaxed linen curtains, checked black and white Catalan throws, willow pendant lights, warm tobacco-coloured velvet chairs from Portobello Market, and limed oak cabinetry and floorboards. Spencer has cleverly designed furniture to fit the proportions of the spaces, with narrow, clean-lined sofas covered in tactile vintage hemp in both the sitting room and upstairs office, and streamlined coffee tables, which encourage more opportunities for display.

Light is also of great importance: 'In the morning, it streams onto the kitchen worktops and by late afternoon the sun hits the table in the first-floor study,' says Spencer. 'I like to follow it around throughout the day – painting and drawing. It has a huge influence on my work.'

Never without a sketchbook, Spencer is always spontaneously capturing a moment, view or object, such as the formation of a seed, the intricate grain of a piece of wood, the rise of a mountain landscape, the movement of trees or the shape of a branch. 'I like to keep a record of inspirations as they occur – and they often form the basis of a solution, an idea for a room or a piece of furniture. I use whatever natural materials are to hand to make those marks: water from a lake, natural soil pigments, clay, grass and often clumps of moss or tied twig branches as a brush – it grounds me to a place and preserves the memory of an observation, idea or time.' It comes as no surprise to learn that in recent years Spencer has also become highly respected for his covetable abstract artworks.

'There is a simplicity and resourcefulness that comes with natural beauty. It nourishes us and has immensely influenced the way we have designed our home. Nature has helped us to view things differently – a privilege that we respect and feel strongly about protecting.'

MONOCHROME STYLE

In the kitchen, a striking artwork, *La Mela e la Pera* by Enzo Mari, was chosen from Teresa's shop, Hedgehog. It is offset by ceramic pendant lights, a collaboration between Spencer and the ceramicist Jo Davda at Brickett Davda. Spencer also designed the kitchen and oak stools.

ORGANIZED DISPLAY

Kitchen shelves display highly organized collections of vases, bottles, glassware and pewter plates. Self-confessed obsessive collectors, the couple's favourite haunts include Portobello Road and Golborne Road in London, but they admit that their cupboards and shelves are now full.

A LOVE OF LINEN

Spencer's sofa, which he originally
designed for Joseph Ettedgui, is covered
in antique Hungarian linen. The black-
and-white cushions from Niki Jones
add textural interest. Spencer custom-
made the bookcase, which is home
to framed seaweeds, an oil painting
by Josep Gerona and a treasured
watercolour by daughter Aurelia.

GROWN-UP RETREAT

Above the piano is a treasured painting
by Llorenç Roviras, Teresa's late father.
Bespoke cabinetry flanking the central
fireplace conceals books and glassware.
The Rush Matters rug complements
the oak-stained coffee table and rustic
oak block, both by Spencer, while the
pair of antique French chairs contribute
timeworn appeal.

WORKING PARTNERSHIP

The couple are very in tune with each other about
decisions relating to the house and enjoy sharing
the ground-floor study. Inherited from Teresa's
family, the partners desk is home to many unique
finds. The modern settle, which Spencer designed,
has cleverly concealed storage built into the base.
Its oak and linen finishes complement the off-white
limestone plaster walls.

Styling Inspiration

— FROM SPENCER & TERESA'S HOME —

TEXTURAL LAYERS

- Collections of papers, vintage scale weights and a selection of artworks and etchings by Spencer and his son Lawrence add tactile interest.
- A warm charcoal throw from The White Company makes a comfortable wrap on cold autumnal days.
- The braided hemp rug and wicker tray heighten the relaxed rustic edge.

HEIRLOOM TREASURES

- Timeless natural and heirloom pieces are favoured over more expensive designer buys, including an iron from Teresa's childhood.
- Branch segments have been collected by Spencer to make organic wall hooks.
- Collections are united by a love of texture, palette and an organic appreciation of nature.

COLOURS & SHAPES

- Striking in its simplicity is the dried hydrangea from the couple's garden, displayed in a vintage demijohn.
- The palette of the off-white limestone plaster walls is repeated in the antique shell.
- An abstract artwork leaning against the wall echoes the lines and colours of the vignette.

THE ART OF SIMPLICITY

With all clothes kept in a separate dressing room, the master
bedroom is a lesson in keeping things simple and uncluttered.
The natural limed oak floor and bedhead promote a sense of
calm and serenity, and this architectural simplicity is matched
by soft white bed linens, subtle ceramic lamps and a soothing
collection of pebbles.

MONOCHROME CONTRASTS

In the bathroom, the Carrara marble
surfaces and Dornbracht hardware lend
a sophisticated feel, tempered by the
natural sponge, a gift from a friend in
Greece, and the coral, which was a lucky
find at a car boot sale. On the facing wall,
an ink drawing by Teresa's brother Pau
Roviras complements the organic feel of
the sea fern and starfish, bought at local
Portobello Market.

Coastal Calm

Not all homeowners choose to design their own spaces. Many prefer instead to work collaboratively with a designer whose creative eye they trust, to guide them through the often overwhelming process. This beautiful new-build home in Cornwall offers valuable insight into just what can be achieved when the owner–designer relationship becomes intuitive and the boundaries of possibility are pushed.

Acclaimed interior designer Marion Lichtig was invited on board at the very start of this project, having worked with the owners on previous properties. The family were keen to build a private escape in the coastal village of Rock and purchased a plot of land that sits centrally in an Area of Outstanding Natural Beauty, overlooking the Camel Estuary. Marion worked closely with project architect Duncan Mackenzie, of Mackenzie Wheeler, to help them create a country-meets-coastal home that would blend seamlessly with the nuances of the vernacular architecture.

'Growing up in Cornwall, the husband had a deep connection to this area and was keen to ensure the new structure harmonized with, not detracted from, the view. The use of honest local materials was an important prerequisite of their build,' says Marion. For the exterior, granite lintels were offset with earthy-coloured basalt stone, echoing the palette of the landscape and rugged coastal garden. Internally, reclaimed Delabole slate used in the hallway connects to the silvery-grey Douglas fir floorboards from Dinesen, uniting the spaces with a soft, textural elegance.

'It is important to me that interior choices respect the architectural style of the building, and the bones of the house are always the starting point. I like to create a calm, consistent canvas that flows throughout in muted

WELCOME HOME
In the hallway, the different textures provided by the mix of wood, slate, simple panelling and patina-rich antiques add immense warmth to the space, while the ceilings clad in weathered oak battens introduce character and age. The inviting antique sofa provides extra seating, and the adjacent boot room ensures the space remains clutter-free.

off-white hues,' says Marion. Indeed, Quiet White, from Papers and Paints, has become Marion's trademark wall colour, which she matches with brighter white ceilings for a gentle change of pace. 'Spaces are then layered with decorative finds, textural fabrics, art and occasional bursts of pattern and colour. Although incorporating elements of the past, rooms should always look as though they belong to the present,' says Marion.

Marion's reputation for sourcing exquisite antiques and reupholstering furniture with collectable vintage textiles is what attracted her client, back in 2000. 'We understood each other's style, and decisions between us became instinctive. It takes time to source the right pieces, and when you find something special, you have to be quick,' says Marion. 'My clients understood the need to think ahead, and we started their collection of individual finds early on in the build. Often it is one statement piece that acts as the foundation for a whole room, so we rented a lock-up and started squirrelling finds away.'

'As the three-year build evolved, we planned where each of these beautiful pieces was going to be placed. It enabled us to create a slow and thoughtful story that feels as if it has been curated over many years,' says Marion. 'Having previously favoured modern furniture, it has been lovely to nurture my clients' new-found love of antiques, and I have enjoyed seeing their own eye evolve since we have finished this project.'

The ground floor opens up from the central hallway into the main, light-filled family spaces, with French doors in the drawing room and kitchen–dining area allowing far-reaching views to the invigorating coastline. Upstairs, five bedrooms – three en-suite – enjoy an unrivalled aspect across to Padstow Harbour.

Elements of surprise but also a regard for symmetry feature inherently in this home too, like the unexpected flower arranging room that leads off the boot room adjacent to the hall. And then there is the hidden 'his and her' dressing room in the master bedroom, which is reached via two unassuming doorways either side of the bed. 'I like things to be ordered and pared back, but storage is always tucked away or decorative, never obvious.'

The contemporary yet classic Bulthaup kitchen and stainless-steel worktops were chosen by Marion to complement the new build. 'With the space and effervescent light, I felt it needed something edgier but a design that would also remain timeless.' The modern style is matched by an oversized, custom-made dining table – designed by Marion with cohesive Dinesen floorboards – which can be divided into two.

In the drawing room, a 19th-century Swedish armoire steals the show, along with a Georgian armchair with a sloping back, re-covered in antique linen. 'I like to juxtapose decorative details with simpler, more linear shapes,' says Marion, referencing the bespoke clean-lined sofa. 'I enjoy mixing antiques of different eras and styles, each piece united by palette or covered in natural vintage linens.' Throughout the house, a few subtle nautical touches are a sophisticated nod to life by the sea, such as a favourite 19th-century, scalloped-back chair in the drawing room and, on the upstairs landing, a vast antique wooden shell – a piece that Marion simply could not resist.

It comes as no surprise that Marion grew up among a family of high-end fashion designers. Her covetable style has that effortless quality that takes time, experience and a certain amount of je ne sais quoi to finesse. After studying fashion at London's Central Saint Martins, she allowed her true love of interiors to come to the fore, 30 years ago, and has never looked back. 'Interiors are about creating an atmosphere – the combination of antiques, rugs, newer finds, fabrics, scent and indigenous flowers makes a space feel welcoming, personal and cosy,' says Marion.

Outside, the lower deck is dressed with weathered tables and chairs that face out to sea, adjacent to a 19th-century cottage that came with the land. Renovated and decorated by Marion in the same pared-back style, it is used as overflow for family guests and can also be rented on request.

The home acts as a daily reminder of the importance of our natural world and just how much nature informs the quality of our spaces. 'The build feels as if it has always belonged. Surrounded by such beauty it was a privilege to work on this project and with clients who share the same passion for integrity and authenticity.'

LAYERS OF WHITE

The drawing room is a wonderful example of how
Marion uses multiple layers of white in patina-rich
tones and textures, to create a room and visual story
that is full of inspiration and provenance. She sourced
the antique finds from a number of London dealers and
The Decorative Antiques and Textiles Fair.

Styling Inspiration

— FROM MARION'S CLIENT PROJECT —

SIMPLICITY & FORM

- Displays work best in odd numbers, and here the power of three is used to great effect with a collection of old ceramic vessels.
- Simple garden branches are introduced seasonally to reflect the changing colours of the landscape beyond.
- Throughout the house, Marion has mixed collections of inexpensive and more decorative, high-end fabrics. At this small window, a simple linen blind is all that is needed.

SENSORY APPEAL

- An antique sofa covered in tactile antique linen is the perfect spot for relaxing and enjoying the coastal views.
- The earthy textures of the blanket complement the modern rustic look, and invite family and guests to make themselves at home.
- A charming metal side table adds a glamorous edge, complemented by the Autumn scented candle from The White Company.

SIGNATURE STYLE

- A beautiful 18th-century Swiss hallway table, from Hilary Batstone Antiques in London, adds statement impact against the all-white backdrop.
- The 19th-century Italian mirror, with its heavily foxed original glass, gives a soft and timeless depth to the calming interior.
- The glow of tealights, a textured lamp and simple autumnal branches make the space feel immediately welcoming.

A MODERN MIX

The contemporary white Bulthaup kitchen contrasts
with the prevalence of antiques in the rest of the house
and introduces a clean-lined accent that complements
the new-build home. Stainless-steel worktops and a
kitchen island topped with Dinesen floorboards display
collections of vintage chopping boards and autumn
gourds, bringing a lived-in, rustic edge to the space.

ROOM WITH A VIEW
Optimizing the wonderful
natural light was a key consideration for the
project. French doors and an abundance of
windows fill the main living areas with light and
unrestricted coastal views. The contemporary table and
timeless Eames chairs are offset by the classic hoop-back
chair from HOWE, rustic beams, ceramics and foliage.

NATURAL TEXTURES

Fallen tree branches from the garden, surrounding open fields and wild
hedgerows are used to create colourful seasonal displays. Foliage is
hung simply from the beams and displayed in antique ceramics sourced
by Marion. Simple, English wooden chairs make charming silhouettes
against the whitewashed walls.

RUSTIC & WILD

Weathered wooden furniture and wicker seating
complement the rugged landscape and add an earthiness
to the patio area leading out from the kitchen. Dried
hydrangea heads from the garden are a pretty autumnal
touch and enhance the relaxed outdoor table setup – the
perfect spot to take in the view.

NATURE'S BOUNTY
The rugged exterior of the house,
designed by Duncan Mackenzie,
of Mackenzie Wheeler, blends
seamlessly with the surrounding
wild coastal landscape. The garden,
by Natalie Ashbee, enhances the
rustic architectural style and blends
effortlessly with the natural setting.

AUTUMNAL LUNCH

— THE ART OF OCCASION —

Autumn is a spectacular season when the leaves begin to turn and nature works its magic. Trees are heavy with ripe pears and apples, while underfoot we walk on carpets of frosty fallen leaves.

We enjoy getting cosy, wrapped up in warm scarves and big jumpers, and begin to hunker down again around welcoming fires, under warm throws. Our homes become cocooning and snug, filled with soft lamplight, which helps to deflect from the short days and early nightfall.

The air fills with the woody aromas of burning logs, scented candles and the welcome return of Sunday roasts. On warmer days, there is still the chance to enjoy the last outdoor lunches of the year, surrounded by nature in all its beauty.

STYLING DETAILS

— AUTUMNAL LUNCH —

SEASONAL COLOUR

- Use foraged finds from your own garden or from the surrounding landscape to dress your table in the style of the season.
- On cold autumn days, this vibrant autumnal palette brings a warmth and cheerful ambience to a relaxed outdoor setup.
- Add layers of seasonal vegetables and soft candlelight – the colourful pumpkins and gourds reflected in the mercury glass tealight holders will enhance the glow.

FIRESIDE GLOW

- The opportunity for spontaneous outdoor lunches is made all the more inviting with sheepskin-covered chairs and a firepit of crackling logs.
- Choose sweet-scented fruitwood logs to burn – apple, pear or cherry will produce a wonderful seasonal aroma and increase the autumnal feel.
- Have lanterns in a range of heights to make the candlelight even more atmospheric. Use them inside the home when temperatures drop.

RAW TEXTURES

- Work with the weathered surfaces of your garden furniture, making them a feature of relaxed outdoor lunches.
- Complementary rustic textures on napkins, placemats and sheepskin cushions enhance the modern rustic feel.
- Red wine in simple ribbed glasses brings additional colour to the autumnal setting.

CALMING INFLUENCE

In the upstairs hallway, a soothing palette of French greys adds textural appeal to the antique chair and chest of drawers. The heavily patinated mirror, with its lightly foxed glass, reflects a set of black-and-white coastal prints, while a simple display of twigs provides sculptural beauty.

TONE ON TONE

Cocooning layers of bed linen from The White Company are finished with a tonal patterned cushion, bringing a tactile warmth to the pared-back room. Simple sketches are matched with mercury glass lamps with pleated white linen shades. The unique antique pendant is a glamorous addition.

DEFINING DETAILS

In the light and airy bathroom, the softly weathered
floorboards continue through to the custom-made
vanity, creating a feeling of cohesion and calm,
while the adjacent Italian limestone bathtub gives
a luxurious finish. At the top of the stairs, a hand-
carved antique shell creates statement impact and
echoes the surrounding natural materials.

Artistic Licence

— A BUCOLIC BARN —

Elsa Mia Elphick and David Cooper are names that you may not have heard of – intentionally operating under the radar. However, for those in the know in the worlds of fashion and art, both are regarded as quiet forces of nature. Elsa, a fashion design graduate from the University of Westminster, began her career as a fashion designer at Alexander McQueen, and over the last 20 years has been a creative director for both independent and leading high-street names. David, with a Master's in Fashion Design from London's Central Saint Martins, worked as the Menswear Creative Director for Alexander McQueen in the early 2000s before founding his own cult fashion wholesale company, P.O. Box No 27715.

When 9/11 struck, international buying teams stopped travelling, and the factory producing David's next collection went into receivership, causing the couple to lose everything overnight. David transitioned into antique furniture, opening The Last Room, a furniture and lifestyle shop in London, which led to interior design commissions for film and fashion names. Then he stepped back from it all and made the decision to return to his fine art roots as a performance artist, sculptor and filmmaker.

'We met at McQueen's in the late '90s and immediately felt like soul mates,' reveals Elsa. Their design styles were in high demand, and their rare, non-egocentric attitudes – 'doers, not talkers'– drew them together in an industry where showy and pretentious were the norm. For them both, home sits at the centre of their creativity: Elsa – creative, commercial and a fanatical minimalist; David – visionary, altruistic and a self-confessed hoarder. Happy in their own company, their polarized styles bring about an artful tension that pushes their individual creative boundaries.

NEW LEASE OF LIFE

Framing the super-stylish, new-build barn is a tall
horse chestnut tree. To the left, there is an orchard full
of old fruit trees. Elsa chose the mature potted lilac tree
at the front entrance for its sculptural elegance and
lichen-covered gnarly branches.

After years of working their magic on rental properties in Paris, Milan, London, Hove and, more recently, London's Bethnal Green, the couple decided to buy their first home, in Suffolk, in 2017. 'We wanted to get away from the city and enjoy a more open, rural way of life,' says Elsa. 'I grew up in Wales, and David in Yorkshire, but my Granny and Mum have been in Suffolk for years and we both knew and loved the area. With all of David's studio pieces, and also for financial reasons, we had always rented warehouse spaces to live in, so in making the move to Suffolk we knew we could neither afford a grand, sprawling house nor live in a tiny cottage. Potential for both home and studio was a prerequisite,' says Elsa.

Located in a quiet, rural hamlet, the authentic two-bedroom, weather-boarded barn replaced a previously dilapidated structure. It had been designed by their neighbours, with the help of a local architect, and was built simply from found and reclaimed materials. 'Previously used as an antiques showroom, the change of use and restrictive covenants had deterred a lot of people – which led to our good fortune,' says Elsa.

The welcoming barn opens into a large, square living space, with a downstairs cloakroom and kitchen–dining area at the rear. Upstairs, two bedrooms have been built into the eaves, along with a bathroom and cleverly concealed storage. Antique and recycled pieces work both decoratively and functionally: 'Even the boot of our car doubles as an extended wardrobe, and an old water tank as a jumper store – we have to be innovative.' Outside in the garden, David has built a self-contained studio from salvaged materials, and together they have transformed the garden from an empty plot to a wonderfully wild, rural haven that acts as an additional living space.

Throughout their home, poured-concrete floors are paired with aged terracotta tiles and reclaimed floorboards, while repurposed Crittall windows and a wood burner, which came from their neighbour's farmhouse, give provenance and a timeworn, weathered appeal. 'Most things in the barn have been discovered, hoarded, rediscovered and displayed in new ways,' says Elsa. 'Many decorative pieces were bought from clearance sales and local dealer Dix-Sept Antiques, along with great finds from Punch the Clock and The Peanut Vendor, in east London – including our favourite coffee table.'

The immensely individual interior follows a calm, natural palette, with the walls painted in Limestone and deep brown Furrow, by Little Greene. There is an abundance of textures, and the eye is drawn to numerous vignettes, collections and groupings that showcase how the alchemy of a small space can feel inspired at every turn. In the brightness of the early morning sun, the palette looks fresh and earthy, but by early afternoon, in the throes of autumn, it is taken over by atmospheric shadows, which highlight a world of contrast and the suggestion of something deeper and more meaningful.

Despite the simplicity, the barn acts as a symbiotic shell for the overlapping worlds of home, work and life. David's paintings and sculptures form part of an ever-changing curation of his work, which is displayed throughout – an integral and rigorous stage in the creative process. His work is so much more than the perceived pared-back canvases. They are full of hidden visual meanings, with David intent on bringing often difficult messages to the fore.

What is clear with both Elsa and David is that they inadvertently challenge you to think more curiously, and to delve a little further below the surface of what you see as you enter their home.

Paintings and sculptures, created using layers of discarded objects, old paint materials, handmade marks and sprayed graffiti, express ideas behind the desperation of institutional life. David's non-autobiographical works and sculptures raise broader political and societal issues that are so often brushed under the carpet, and explore the importance of nurturing self-worth, pride and personal value.

Home stands as a metaphor for a place that you love and feel loved in – but that is not always everyone's norm. The presence of David's work in this comfortable home acts as a pertinent reminder of the importance of conscience and community, and the danger of indifference. David was chosen as one of only ten early career sculptors globally for The Gilbert Bayes Award 2021 by The Royal Society of Sculptors; it feels as if his voice is being heard.

Styling Inspiration

SHADOW PLAY

- At night, shadows cast by candlelight play on the natural walls, creating depth and mystery.
- Soft candlelight illuminates sculptural artworks, while the Pomegranate scented candle from The White Company is soothing and inviting.
- Simple foraged grasses in a glass vase are reflected onto the walls, adding to the ethereal feel of the home.

WRAP UP

- The sitting room is dressed with tactile, earthy-coloured throws and inviting cushions.
- A soft, white wool rug introduces an autumnal layer of warmth to the cool, concrete floor and increases the sense of comfort.
- Invitingly low, linen-covered seating encourages you to unwind when the nights become colder and longer.

WEATHERED EDGE

- The charm of perfectly imperfect surfaces shows in pieces marked by time, such as a bench mended with a rusty nail or screw marks on an old table.
- A natural palette of worn canvas, battered wood and handmade white ceramics lends a relaxed, lived-in and loved vibe.
- Delicate, earthy grasses juxtapose harder-hitting touches of green in David's work *White Wall*.

NATURAL HUES

Since moving to the country, both Elsa and David have
nurtured a love of plants and gardening. The black wooden
table is offset with different raw textures and thriving green
indoor plants. The patina-rich old school cupboard at the
back of the kitchen replaced a corner unit.

STORAGE & DISPLAY

The kitchen, designed by the previous owners, includes a
mix of white-painted wooden cabinetry and simple linen
curtains. Stylish, hand-forged creations have replaced the
original hardware, while a decorative peg rail displays all
manner of kitchenalia.

SHADES OF WHITE

In the downstairs cloakroom, a reclaimed white butler sink has been repurposed as a cloakroom vanity. Combined with aged brass taps, a driftwood tray shelf and dried garden flowers, they create an earthy and natural look.

ADDING THE EDGE

In the guest bedroom, frilled white linen sheets stand out against the darker walls, imparting a soft, feminine elegance. A simple linen panel makes an affordable curtain treatment. The rush-seated chair adds textural interest.

GET CREATIVE

The interior of the corrugated-iron garden studio has
been clad with the riveted insides of an old water tank,
and pieced together with salvaged York stone and
reclaimed Crittall windows. Planted with a profusion of
fig and olive trees, herbs, verbena and various grasses,
the garden is a wonderful place to enjoy a leisurely
autumn lunch.

AUTUMN HOME RITUALS

Once temperatures begin to cool, the days become shorter and
the glorious colours of autumn return, our lives start to move back indoors.
Thoughts turn to layering up our home, the prospect of warming, homemade
meals and the delight of hunkering down around a roaring fire.
I am always excited to get cosy again, and these favourite rituals
really add to the comfort at home.

As open doors are closed and curtains drawn,
it is time to store away lightweight summer
linens, cushions and breezy bunting and make our
favourite spaces feel cosy.

•

Place soft throws over chair arms and sofas and
introduce more tactile, knitted cushions, for a sense
of warmth, softness and comfort.

•

Have chimneys swept, stack the log pile and fill
pretty baskets or bowls with fireside kindling.

•

Swap summer foliage for gorgeous autumnal
finds or begin to mix it in. Think berries, earthy
ferns and leafy branches.

•

Restyle surfaces for the season and use pieces that
bring a gentle softness: tactile pebbles, hand-thrown
ceramic lamps and vases, along with deep-pile rugs
and touches of rustic basketwork.

•

Reposition lamps to make darker corners more
inviting. Dimmers always set the right tone and
prevent spaces feeling too bright and sterile.

For intimate suppers, opt for napkins and
placemats that are soft to the touch, and introduce
lots of layered candlelight.

•

I move onto richer, warmer notes for candle
and room diffuser scents – everything from
pomegranate, cassis and oakmoss through to amber,
cedar and sandalwood.

•

In our bedrooms, we return to a lightweight duvet
and comfortable layers. A bed always looks its
best with a bedspread and lovely throw across the
bottom, which serves as a wonderful extra layer too.

•

Re-evaluate bathrooms and check their spa-like
status for the colder days ahead! Enjoy a good
declutter and switch to more nurturing bath treats,
as well as softer, heavier towels and robes.

•

Make the most of the last, clear autumnal nights
snuggled up around a warming log brazier, with
piles of outdoor knitted throws at the ready and
atmospheric candle lanterns lighting the way.

•

Towards the end of autumn, I always check my
wrapping and ribbons drawer, as Christmas planning
is now just around the corner.

IV

WINTER

Old Meets New

— A TIMELESS MEWS —

The discerning eye of Karen and Anthony Cull have become synonymous internationally with their understated interiors style and highly regarded antiques business, Anton & K. The couple's curation of 18th-, 19th- and 20th-century finds – predominantly Swedish, French and Belgian – is compelling, and in recent years this has combined with a passion for more abstract art and ceramics. At home, their intuitive approach to sourcing coalesces with how they choose to decorate their own spaces: timeless, individual and always evolving. 'We buy only what we love – it is always about whether a piece feels special, or has that unexplainable, elusive appeal,' says Karen.

With their main home in the heart of the rural Cotswold countryside, the couple decided a few years ago to look for a nearby bolthole, as a more urban escape. Their charming, single-level mews house is located in the beautiful spa town of Cheltenham, renowned as one of the most complete Regency towns in Britain. Just a 30-minute drive from home, this three-year-old property, built using reclaimed bricks, is tucked in a quiet back street, a short walk to fashionable Montpellier and historic Pittville Park. It is the perfect spot from which to enjoy friendly local restaurants, cafes, concerts and unique independent stores.

The decoration of Karen and Anthony's mews home is a masterclass in how to make the most of a small space, with minimal rooms creating maximum impact. Crittall-style doors frame views from the kitchen, and the sitting room and bedroom over an unexpected, whitewashed courtyard. The private outdoor area successfully fuses old and new: an antique French table topped with trademark Belgian blue stone, matched with

BLACK & WHITE

Old meets new in the monochrome dining room, converted from
a second bedroom. Removing the partition wall now connects
the space to the main living area. Walls painted in Strong White, by
Farrow & Ball, are matched with Gervasoni Ghost 05 armchairs,
by Paola Navone, which offset darker antique finds.

clean-lined contemporary furniture from Paris-based Ronan & Erwan Bouroullec and 18th-century rustic Chinese stools. Stone planters filled with *Osmanthus* x *burkwoodii* and ferns (see pages 190–1) reference the couple's love of nature, which is reinforced inside the home by displays of simple bare branches and twigs reflecting the skeletal forms of winter.

Indoors, finds are anchored by their perfectly imperfect finishes: 'We have always been drawn to pieces that show the marks of time,' says Karen. 'Softly worn edges and patina-rich surfaces resonate with us both – it shows a sense of history and provenance that means pieces have been loved, handled and used.' There is intrigue behind each find, and by mixing antiques with more contemporary pieces, new life is given to old treasures, at the same time adding depth and character to modern, box-shaped rooms.

Throughout their home, the couple play with an artful mix of scale: in the dining room – a former second bedroom – an oversized black Gustavian cupboard adds statement impact in the low-ceilinged space with layered displays of white ceramics: 1970s East German designs alongside favourites from Astier de Villatte and earthy mid-century finds. On the 1970s Angelo Mangiarotti travertine dining table, the couple's favourite piece, a substantial 19th-century Chinese water pot stands alongside finer Gunnar Nylund mid-century ceramics, part of a larger collection curated on the mantelpiece and coffee table.

Informal, white linen-covered dining chairs have an ethereal feel and are complemented by contemporary Serge Mouille wall lights and an abstract painting by Mallorcan artist Jaume Roig, whom the couple discovered when they lived on the island.

Minimal whitewashed rooms exude a feeling of calm and restraint that allows statement furniture – such as the white, mid-century Paradis sofa by Kerstin Hörlin-Holmquist, and a narrow mid-century rope sofa, in the style of Audoux-Minet – the space it deserves to breathe.

Over the fireplace, the 1970s Swedish panelled mirror creates the illusion of increased depth, while reflecting select finds around the room, including an 18th-century Swedish cupboard and a treasured 1950s black and white painting.

Abstract artwork features everywhere in this home, cleverly drawing the eye into spaces that have less opportunity for substantial display.

The pared-back vibe continues into the breakfast area, where a large, 18th-century Swedish cupboard (see page 193) provides valuable storage for artisanal tableware and glassware, carefully chosen by Karen. This decorative piece of furniture contrasts with the linear, more modern kitchen units that came with the house. Karen and Anthony have instinctively overlaid their own mark on the kitchen design by adding antique patterned wall tiles, to complement the utilitarian marble worksurfaces, and updating hardware with hand-forged cast-iron replacements. Their tactile simplicity is aesthetically pleasing and acts as a nod to the prevailing monochrome tones.

The many rustic pieces in the home include early Swedish folk art bowls, displayed on a French garden console, repurposed as a casual kitchen island. Original Hans Wegner chairs in the adjacent breakfast area frame the 1950s Eero Saarinen table. Their natural rush seats echo the raw materials elsewhere: sisal rugs, looped wool carpets, a rush headboard and welcoming bed linens, all enhancing the feeling of laid-back comfort. 'Everything is used, loved and enjoyed,' says Karen.

A cleverly concealed laundry and pantry room, tucked in the corner of the kitchen, and new built-in storage in the master bedroom allow small spaces to retain their charm and feeling of calm. 'As soon as we arrive, we relax,' says Karen. 'We fell in love with the mews and its seamless connection to the outdoor courtyard. In winter, our home is filled with natural light and when the afternoons draw in early, we enjoy lighting candles and taking the time to cosy up, read and unwind,' says Karen.

This home is a lesson in how small, quiet spaces can leave a bold and lasting impression – where inspiration sits at the heart of it all. Karen and Anthony's gift for buying antiques is encouragement for us all to choose only the things that make the heart sing, and to be judicious in those choices. At the end of the day, the thrill of finding just the right piece is always worth the wait.

DOUBLE VISION

In the corner of the dining room, a 19th-
century French butcher's marble-topped
table is used for writing and work. The foxed,
panelled mirror enhances the feeling of
space and reflects the simple branches that
complement the tones of the abstract painting
by Jaume Roig opposite.

ARTFUL SIMPLICITY

Throughout the house, collections of weathered antiques sit comfortably
alongside modern art. Abstract Spencer Fung prints decorate the wall above
the mid-century rope sofa, while treasured ceramics are displayed on the 1970s
travertine coffee table. Scented candles and soft lantern light brighten the
winter mood and enhance the restful ambience.

INSIDE OUT

The compact brick courtyard has been whitewashed to bounce light back
into the home, while a circular mirror reflects the sitting room interior
and increases the sense of outdoor space. New wooden plank flooring
continues the flow of natural materials, and decorative antique pots and
urns heighten the impact of lush plant displays.

Styling Inspiration

— FROM KAREN & ANTHONY'S HOME —

ROUGH WITH THE SMOOTH

- Tactile antiques soften the clean lines of the kitchen and give personality and provenance to this new-build space.
- Simple Spanish and Swedish antiques add a timeworn elegance to everyday occasions. Nothing is saved for best, with each piece chosen for both practicality and beauty.
- A French garden table has the perfect proportions for the compact kitchen space and creates a desirable prep-table-meets-island.

MONOCHROME LAYERS

- Reclaimed antique tiles add visual interest as a kitchen splashback.
- The simple lines of the earthy teapot and cups enhance the modern rustic feel, while bringing a quiet elegance to a daily ritual.
- The angular chopping boards accentuate the monochrome palette of the kitchen.

NATURAL ELEGANCE

- The light-filled breakfast area features 18th-century antiques alongside mid-century modern finds. White and neutral tones balance the eclectic styles for an informal, welcoming feel.
- Simple branches of pine bring the outside in, their heady scent hinting at the seasonal festivities to come.
- A natural rug lends a warm softness underfoot and creates a more intimate, atmospheric feel in the functional kitchen area.

RELAX & REST

The bedroom is layered with softly striped cushions from Caravane
and appealing bed linens, textural knits and soft ribbed jacquards from
The White Company. Gentle textures, including the rush headboard,
dry-scraped footstool, and rustic, 18th-century, authentic Chinese
elm worker stools, combine to create a restful ambience. The lighting
and abstract paintings by Jaume Roig add a more contemporary edge.

Weathered Sophistication

Creating a home that comes with atmosphere is all about first impressions. Does it move you? Does it feel at one with its natural surroundings? That immediate uplifting impression is one that Chrissie and Nick have fostered in their Buckinghamshire home. They discovered the house 16 years ago and have spent the intervening years slowly evolving it. Chrissie explains that, with four children now in their late teens and early twenties, 'It's the place where we can all simply be ourselves and enjoy time together.'

'At The White Company we talk a lot about creating things for today, tomorrow and for ever, and I feel the same about our home. The evolution of a home never really finishes – it's always ongoing, a combination of planned major changes, maintenance projects and spontaneous subtle tweaks.'

The Pool House, located away from the main house, sits within a magical walled garden. 'When we moved here, this area was home to a very large and neglected kitchen garden. We wanted to reinvent it, for it to become more manageable and special – a space where we could enjoy time together at weekends and in the holidays. We treat it as a technology-free zone: somewhere to read, think, play tennis, swim, attempt to grow vegetables and flowers, and enjoy slow lunches or fun suppers with family and friends.'

The entrance to the walled garden is through a small, charming loggia – a converted outbuilding in the stable yard, with aged herringbone-brick floors, raw panelled walls and a wonderful sense of scale, which sets the tone of the Pool House that follows. 'I always love walking through the loggia and up the connecting pathway. Framed by cherry trees and sculptural box balls, it is the antithesis of our fast-paced, day-to-day lives in London. With the original, red brick walls surrounding the garden, it feels wonderfully protected and peaceful.'

FESTIVE WELCOME

At the entrance to the walled garden leading to the Pool House, former garden buildings have been given a new lease of life. Rich textures abound with weathered brick floors and untreated timber panelling. A simple wooden bench, an oversized natural wreath and the glow of lanterns add a rustic, festive welcome for family and guests.

The brief for the design of the Pool House was for a contemporary structure that would blend quietly within the natural space. Weathered beautifully over time, the now-silvery grey, oak-clad steel frame feels as if it has always belonged. Vast sliding glass doors, on opposite sides of the building, provide a seamless flow from the new stone pool terrace into the Pool House itself and through to the tennis court on the other side. 'On cooler days, the doors remain closed, but we are still able to enjoy unobstructed views. That sense of it feeling lived-in and at one with the garden was very important to us. Fashion comes and goes, but a connection to nature is always timeless.'

'In spring, summer and early autumn, the doors and skylights are always open and it feels as if you are part of the garden, while in the midst of winter, the view becomes more sculptural and pared-back. When the leaves start to come off the trees and the days turn colder, the interior takes on a new cocooning feel – the central, concrete fire burns steadily throughout the day, and the relaxing aroma of scented candles feels uplifting.'

The design process was a collaborative one. Chrissie worked alongside architects Michaelis Boyd on the exterior, and designer Rose Uniacke on the interior, while Nick worked closely with the family's gardener, Phil, and their landscape architect Robert Myers, to reinvent the walled garden.

The structure, made up of the main open-plan living, dining and kitchen areas, incorporates a separate spa area and a small Pilates studio and gym on the upstairs mezzanines. 'Inspiration for the interior was influenced by the garden itself – we wanted it to feel white and natural and the materials to work harmoniously.' Throughout, weathered wooden floorboards are complemented by clean-lined concrete surfaces, which are both practical and stylish. On the walls, Tadelakt, a traditional Moroccan plaster finish, lends a light and airy feel and is incredibly soft, gentle and tactile.

'I've worked with Michaelis Boyd and Rose on a number of projects now and trust their style and judgement implicitly. I particularly love how Rose takes the time to get to know her clients and gets under the skin of their lifestyle. All her projects manage to capture and reflect the style and taste of each homeowner, and she has a fantastic ability to take a space and use its scale and proportions perfectly – something that is very easy to get wrong. With the Pool House, she gave me the confidence to work with new materials and has helped us to create a wonderfully simple interior – perfectly refined, but incredibly comfortable for family life. With four children and three dogs, it was imperative that it not only looked good but worked functionally also.'

'The Pool House comes into its own at Christmas time, too, when we have lots of family to stay. The Christmas tree in the main house is always real, but in the Pool House I cover our 9-foot faux tree with a mass of fairy lights and simple glass baubles. I light copious candles throughout. It is very special.'

'On Christmas Eve, we walk to our local church for carols and then return to the Pool House for mulled wine, mince pies and Christmas jazz. The terrace comes to life with lanterns and warming outdoor log braziers, and the outdoor sofas are dressed with cosy sheepskins and soft wool throws. A relaxed and simple family supper always follows around the indoor dining table – one solid piece of oak, made from a tree that fell in our garden. Designed by Rose, it has gentle edges and a wonderfully weathered surface. It has been at the heart of family life for a long time and holds many precious memories for us all.'

'While we enjoy supper, the dogs curl up on the sofas around the fire – it's chaotic, life-affirming and the best start to Christmas. On a clear night, with the stars out, it really couldn't be more magical, and is one of the many reasons it is probably our most favourite place to be.'

UNWIND & RELAX

At the heart of the Pool House, the contemporary hearth and floating concrete chimney encourage everyone to relax and adopt a slower rhythm. Surrounded by deep, comfortable sofas and cosy textiles, the fire gives off a warm glow that complements the soft focus of festive candlelight and twinkly Christmas tree lights.

Styling Inspiration

DECORATIVE SIMPLICITY

- A special collection of glass drops and vintage-style mercury glass baubles decorate the Christmas tree.
- The decorations bounce light around the open-plan space, adding a sophisticated sense of peace and quiet to the festive ambience.
- Numerous twinkly lights make the atmosphere even more magical at night.

WINTER WHITES

- At Christmas, stacks of ivory and neutral textiles, topped with a sprig of pine, add decorative appeal to a cosy corner.
- Extra piles of thick wool throws and soft sheepskins kept to hand ensure guests feel comfortable, warm and at home.
- Natural Tadelakt plaster walls and an aged wooden stool complement the natural textures.

NATURAL PALETTE

- The central concrete fireplace is layered with a tray of decorative tealights for sensory appeal.
- The White Company scent Winter is a favourite at home, but in the Pool House, Pomegranate has become a family tradition in the build-up to Christmas.
- Simple sprigs of greenery and pine enhance the festive feel, while contributing their own subtle fragrance.

CHRISTMAS EVE SUPPER

— THE ART OF OCCASION —

Winter marks a time for slowing down, nesting and allowing ourselves the time to hibernate. Just as nature needs time to rest and recover, so do we. Our homes become cosy, reflective retreats – places for us to unwind, plan and take the time to do the things that often get forgotten during the warmer months.

With the imminent arrival of Christmas, the pace increases, and the frenzy of shopping, gift wrapping and parties takes hold. Our homes take on a new glow as we prepare to welcome family and friends to festive celebrations. Tables are layered with beautiful glassware, plates and linens, and rooms fill with the aroma of seasonal branches and candles.

As the new year begins, nature withdraws yet further. Informal suppers become a welcoming distraction, and vases filled with late-season flowers offer a glimpse of warmer days to come.

STYLING DETAILS

— CHRISTMAS EVE SUPPER —

NATURAL TEXTURES

- Simple concrete vessels containing ivy plants and tall candles create wonderful table centrepieces, which can be easily moved around the home.
- The understated beauty of a timeworn wooden table lets the ceramics and glassware take centre stage.
- Gently ribbed glassware is perfect in a relaxed and rustic setting.

MAKING MEMORIES

- Bring together all your favourite table pieces to create a magical scene that guests will remember.
- Candles have the magical ability to transform the mood, while festive scents, such as aromatic cinnamon sticks and cut spruce sprigs, add their own sensory appeal.
- Personalize place settings with handwritten name tags and soft toy table gifts for children.

FINAL TOUCHES

- Vary the height of lanterns, tealights and candleholders in a table setting, to attract the eye and increase the impact of the display.
- Nestle a cut-glass lantern into a simple faux wreath embellished with fragrant garden cuttings.
- Use pretty wooden dishes to contain seasonal nuts and treats alongside pretty tealights.

INDOOR–OUTDOOR

Outdoor furniture and occasional jute pouffes,
dressed with various textiles in different shades of
white and grey, provide cosy and informal seating.
Faux fur cushions heighten the feeling of comfort.
Combined with the festive smells of warm mulled
wine, hot mince pies and scented candles, this scene
is the embodiment of Christmas.

Lakeside House

— NEW BEGINNINGS —

For Jane Clark and her husband Mark Copping, the prospect of breathing new life back into the historic stone walls of this beautiful house in Rutland was an opportunity they could not resist. Set on the banks of a picturesque lake, surrounded by mature woodland, the house was built originally in 1880 as three separate workers' cottages. It remained in the hands of one family for hundreds of years, and was transformed in the 1970s to become both a family home and the location of a stand-alone recording studio, frequented by, among others, The Who, Eric Clapton and The Rolling Stones.

'We fell in love with both the setting and the building, and it was important to us that we honoured its integrity,' says Jane, who embarked on a six-month renovation, magically changing whatever was needed to suit modern family living. 'The house is inextricably linked to its natural surroundings, and we wanted the interior to have a greater connection to the landscape and the wonderful light that prevails.' The gothic windows have been kept deliberately curtain-free, allowing views to flow seamlessly into the calming interior, painted in soft natural tones. Meanwhile, Crittall-style wooden screens have replaced sections of solid internal walls, which encourages the light to bounce freely around.

To counter the long and narrow run of the house, the couple established a renewed sense of purpose for each room, to create a home that feels united and fully used. 'For us, a house is just a commodity, but a home is like a partner – spaces need to be connected, to feel loved and relaxed.'

In the central hallway, the original flagstone floors and wide stone staircase have been preserved and carefully matched with new natural materials: marble for worksurfaces, vanities and showers; porcelain tiles

NATURAL CONNECTION

Blending seamlessly with the surrounding landscape, natural materials and an earthy ambience are immediately obvious as you enter the house. Several partition walls have been removed, which increases the feeling of connectivity and flow. During the colder winter months, the Parkray log burner adds an atmospheric and inviting glow.

from Mandarin Stone for kitchen and bathroom floors; and textural, grey tumbled oak for floors in the dining room, sitting room and study. Intended originally as parquet, the floor has been laid in simple vertical strips, which complement the linear feel of newly exposed ceiling joists, to increase the feeling of space throughout.

From the inviting entrance, a double-sided wood burner connects to a relaxed snug and study, dressed with furniture and art chosen over many years – 'pieces that resonated spontaneously, never of-the-moment trend choices'. In the centre of the house, a classic, clean-lined kitchen, designed by Jane and made by British Standard, offsets the decorative arched windows, while a timber-framed banquette creates an intimate nook, layered with Gotland sheepskins, Moroccan cushions and striped linens.

The adjacent dining area – more formal in feel, with a beautiful handmade table by talented maker Matthew Cox – leads into the elegant sitting room, to reveal a mix of antique chairs, including pieces from Claire Langley Antiques and Clignancourt flea market in Paris. 'Our motto is: re-cycle, re-use, re-novate. I like to buy timeless, quality pieces, but when things no longer fit or need changing, I am happy to sell them or give them away. It avoids feeling weighed down by possessions or becoming burdened with the guilt of not letting go – an underused sentiment in an increasingly acquisitive society.'

Natural fabrics add a textural honesty throughout the home: antique, Eastern European linen, sourced by Jane, has been used for upholstery, cushions and bedheads. This blends perfectly with newer de Le Cuona fabrics, jute from The Cloth House in London and a much loved mohair velvet on the custom-made sitting room sofa.

'Mark has made a lot of the mirrors, occasional tables and the sitting room floor lamps. If we can't find what we want, he cleverly designs his own,' says Jane. Equally creative and resourceful, Jane handcrafts luxurious cashmere throws and jumpers from repurposed yarn in her at-home studio. These add a sense of comfort to graceful bedrooms, with their additional layers of crisp white cottons, soft velvets and warm wools.

'Mark and I met 22 years ago: he had sold his design business and was on a stopover in London, en route from South Africa to start a diving school in Belize.' After a serendipitous encounter in Marylebone, Mark never made the connecting flight and the couple have shared a sense of adventure ever since. 'We have enjoyed moving regularly and have renovated multiple period homes in London; a medieval townhouse and rural, vineyard farmhouse in France; and now this wonderful space in Rutland.'

Innately nomadic, curious and creative, the couple both grew up abroad and have experienced a number of diverse cultures and lifestyles. Yet they remain refreshingly grounded, understated and real. 'The move here from London was driven by a need for more open space and a desire to feel closer to both family and the changing seasons. It has fed our souls immeasurably but it has also been instrumental in our decision to re-evaluate our careers and life journey,' says Jane.

Disillusioned with the corporate treadmill and changing social norms, both have paid greater attention to the gentle rhythms of nature and the simplicity that comes with a less competitive way of life. During the Covid-19 lockdown Jane made the decision to close her successful head-hunting business, which sourced global marketers and senior management for top fashion and creative brands. 'The pandemic has taught us that there is never a good time for change – if you want to make something happen, you just have to go for it.'

'We have enjoyed being custodians of this wonderful home but are selling up, to realize our passion for interiors and begin a new career together: buying a small, Grade II listed, derelict cottage, as a nearby investment project – while simultaneously hoping to demystify the process of bringing a listed building into the 21st century – and commencing a longer-term, sustainable build for ourselves, on a shared farmhouse plot, in Portugal,' says Jane. 'In a world that is becoming increasingly robotic, polarized and restrictive, we have a window of opportunity to create something personal and meaningful – which on our own terms feels immensely liberating.'

TEXTURAL FINDS

The minimal kitchen cabinetry is offset by lots of different textural surfaces. An island bench, a repurposed find from friend Anna Valentine, is matched with utilitarian antique stools of wood and metal, while a jute rug from The White Company adds a rustic feel and is cosy underfoot in winter.

VINTAGE INSPIRATION

Reclaimed lights add a sculptural dimension to the kitchen. Those above the AGA, sourced from LASSCO, are from the 1950s and were originally used in the London department store Peter Jones. The reconditioned AGA, from Avec Cookers, is a treasured purchase – half the price of a new model and in perfect condition.

CUSTOM-MADE
Vintage French chairs and favourite
monochrome artworks frame the
custom-made, zinc-topped table.
The prints were bought in a French
market, close to where the couple
used to live. A contemporary
painting by Carl Moore on the right
balances the display.

NATURAL GLOW

The couple's favourite time of day at home is the morning, when the sun weaves its warming, low light throughout the house, illuminating the artworks. The whispering of the trees and the much loved noise of the wild ducks on the lake entice visitors outside even in winter.

GOING WITH THE GRAIN

The dining room enjoys uninterrupted views out to the lake. The wooden table by Matthew Cox is surrounded by chairs found on eBay and, from Jane's great-aunt, a pair of heirloom chairs which Mark has reupholstered. Garden-cut branches complement the rustic table setting.

A CUT ABOVE

The antique sofa, repurposed by antiques dealer Claire Langley, was split in two and given a new central section, to create its oversized length. Painted in Paint & Paper Library's Slate II, the calming walls act as a backdrop to the striking Shona sculpture from Zimbabwe, where Jane used to live

Styling Inspiration

— FROM JANE & MARK'S HOME —

SENSORY PLEASURE

- A flickering fire, scented candles and soft candlelight enhance the cosy winter ambience.
- With comfort a prerequisite for Jane, she has chosen furniture for its ability to cocoon and embrace.
- A reclaimed, beautifully textural pigsty door, discovered in France, has been cleverly remodelled by Mark into a unique, metal-framed coffee table.

DARK & MOODY

- The charcoal fabric weave on the armchair contrasts with the predominantly natural-hued interior and adds depth and texture.
- Soft wool and cashmere throws, in softer tonal shades, encourage you to sit back and relax.
- Rustic sisal carpet anchors the space with a quiet elegance and increases the feeling of warmth and comfort.

RUSTIC DETAILS

- A deconstructed antique chair, reupholstered in jute and linen, adds a natural refined edge.
- The contemporary floor lamp, from Pamono, juxtaposes old with new and helps create the perfect reading corner.
- The sheepskin pouffe from The White Company doubles as a comfortable footrest and useful occasional table.

THOUGHTFUL DESIGN

In the master bedroom, Jane has kept curtain
treatments to a bare minimum, with simple
linen blackout panels, which can be hung
across at night, to highlight the architectural
lines of the window. The sofa, which has been
recovered three times, is one of the first pieces
of furniture that Jane ever bought.

SIMPLE SOPHISTICATION

The restored vintage washstand, found
discarded when the couple moved to their
previous home in France, adds a rustic
touch to the guest bedroom, as do the
branches displayed in a simple white vase.
Textural surfaces in wood, linen and marble
enhance the calming vibe.

QUIET RETREAT

A salvaged door has been used to great
effect as a simple headboard, and the
scallop-edged chair, one of pair that Jane
bought from a junk shop in France, has been
restored and reupholstered. The gallery
wall acts as a visual reminder of homes,
people and places.

WINTER HOME RITUALS

Despite the long dark nights, there is something so very magical
about winter. Along with the cold, crisp and sculptural landscape
comes the season to gather family and friends close. It's time to
create special memories, share old traditions and create new
ones too. These are my favourite rituals for making our home feel
as warm, comfortable and welcoming as possible.

Fill the house with candlelight – whether glowing
tealights, tall elegant pillars or seasonally scented
candles – to lift your spirits as well as your rooms.
My favourite notes include everything from
cinnamon, clove, orange and myrrh through to
eucalyptus, pine, cognac and smoked woods.

•

Restyle coffee tables, surfaces and shelves to
incorporate candlelight and winter foliage. I love to
'create layers' and, as one brilliant stylist taught me,
when you are arranging surfaces, keep it 'simple but
strong', such as a bowl of winter clementines, which
looks so beautiful and impactful.

•

Adding in extra-warm layers ensures your home feels
beautifully dressed for winter. Pile soft velvets and
faux furs, as well as warm sheepskins and super-soft
textural knits, on sofas, benches, chairs and beds.

•

At this time of year, I love everything from potted
heathers, winter pine needles and rustic wintry
branches through to white ranunculus, hyacinths and
tall sculptural amaryllis. Small pots of trailing ivy are
also wonderful for table centre displays.

Fairy lights are particularly magical in winter. Invest
in those with plenty of tiny bulbs and enjoy them all
winter, draped around trees and wound into wreaths.

•

I love to prepare our guest bedrooms, and my
checklist always includes a pretty water carafe and
glass, sleep pillow spray and a sprig of flowers beside
the bed. A hot water bottle and a soft throw on a
beautifully made bed make guests feel special, and I
always add recent magazines, a robe and a hairdryer.

•

Every bed will benefit from the luxury
of a sheepskin mattress topper. They never fail
to lend warmth and blissful comfort.

•

In our guest bathrooms, I enjoy adding nurturing
bath-time treats, piles of soft towels and a scented
candle, along with a basket of might-need essentials
(often collected from hotel stays), such as cotton
wool, a toothbrush, toothpaste, razor and sewing kit.

•

As we edge into the new year, I like to think ahead
to the prospect of warmer days and take inspiration
from Pinterest, Instagram, books, magazines and
stores. In no time at all, spring will be here.

INSPIRATION & RESOURCES

GREAT DESIGN IS NOT JUST VISUAL

When we talk about interiors, we are for the most part considering the architectural design and visual aesthetic of our homes. For me, home is the most important place in the world, and although I love it to look good, how it makes us feel as a family is just as important.

Fundamentally, I am a shopkeeper and product designer, and I make no claim to being an interior designer. However, when it comes to atmosphere, I am intensely aware of what feels good – that elusive sense of being moved by a space and feeling immediately comfortable and at home. It is far more than how a space looks. It is also about how it smells, how things feel, and the behind-the-scenes stories of where things are made.

The type of scent we use in our homes has an extraordinary ability to shift our mood: bright and uplifting, quiet and calming, or cosseting and peaceful. That is why, at The White Company, we love to change our home scents throughout the seasons. What feels right in winter will not evoke the spirit of spring, so we create choices that work in harmony with the natural elements and celebrate the seasonal ebb and flow.

My love of a scented home began many years ago, when I would place tealights under a small bowl of water with a few drops of aromatherapy oil to match my mood. If I needed a lift, I would choose something energizing, or if ready for a good night's sleep (often the case when the children were small), something calming. It made me vitally aware that the atmosphere I created and the scent I chose had a direct impact on how I felt.

Touch and comfort are also key sensory triggers that respond to the seasonal mood. In autumn and winter, I love to dress beds, sofas and benches with lots of super-soft cushions and warm, cosy, textural layers. In spring that changes to lighter, fresher

cottons and beautiful soft linens. Regardless of the season, the luxury of cashmere is an indulgence that never fails to please.

Touch is at the heart of everything we design at The White Company, and we constantly ask ourselves whether every new piece is special enough and if it will be a pleasure to use. I believe passionately that monotonous daily tasks can be elevated by using quality pieces that look great and also feel good to hold: a soft towel to wrap up in when we step out of the bathtub; a chopping board carved from a tactile piece of wood that makes cutting a lemon a pleasure; a tea towel that looks stylish and dries brilliantly; a coffee cup that is both beautiful and comforting to hold; and, of course, sheets that are a joy to lie on at the end of a busy day.

We talk a lot about creating products for today, tomorrow and for ever – and we love to work with artisanal suppliers who are experts in their fields. This feels like a good ethos to have in mind when shopping too. There has never been a more important time to stop disposable purchasing and to avoid fast-fashion home fixes. It is important to take time choosing and invest only in pieces we love. Quality finds that work together can be added to over time and, crucially, will last for many years to come.

Home has never mattered more, and taking the time to make it somewhere we love being is everything. When we master that elusive sense of atmosphere, it helps our shoulders to drop every time we step through the door.

FINDING YOUR PERSONAL STYLE WITH WHITE

All of the homes featured in this book and my first book, *For the Love of White*, have a wonderful harmony that runs through them. Each one illustrates beautifully the many different ways in which to work with white, all of them special and unique. When it comes to creating our own homes, though, not all the interior styles we like will work seamlessly together. So when there are so many choices, how do we navigate our own personal way of using white?

To fine-tune your style, it is important to work out what you need from each space, and to identify what design styles you love or are less keen on. Understanding your needs and preferences early on avoids confusion.

For me, all great home design projects have a strong 'core essence' that fluidly connects spaces and objects. The backdrop foundations begin with ideas for flooring, surfaces, hardware, paint and wallpaper, and these make the decorative decisions that follow much easier.

Tools like Pinterest are really helpful in seeking out ideas, but it is important to have a physical mood board that pulls together foundation ideas, which you can move around your home and view in situ.

I often try to single out one image (no more than three) to sum up the core combination of materials that I am keen to use. The pictures opposite are a good illustration of the type of shots that can help, with each showing a strong sense of personal style.

Once you have decided on your choices for key materials, order in samples and layer them together to check they work in reality – they can be very different from how you imagined them in a picture.

The next step is to choose your preferred white paint. Mine is Slate I from Paint & Paper Library, and in our London home we have used it throughout – on walls, doors, cornices, ceilings and window frames. I love the quiet, harmonious foundation it has created.

There are so many whites to choose from and they look so different from home to home. Always test colours on white paper, never directly on the walls, and paint the sample edge to edge, to avoid reflections that distort the finish.

Overlay your mood board with ideas for decorative finishes: furniture, curtain and upholstery fabrics, lighting and accessories. How you choose to accessorize and dress your spaces will make your home feel unique.

Quality, comfort and practicality are key considerations when choosing furniture, so consider lifestyle needs to determine what is important to you.

Curating the finishing touches is transformative. Simple additions such as an artful display of ceramics, well-placed textiles and layered styling on beds, shelves and tables will heighten the visual appeal.

If you are designing a whole house at once, consider rooms together, to ensure the flow of spaces connects. If you are at the start of a longer, slower project, do not compromise on choices – it is worth getting your core ideas clear at the outset, as this will ensure you achieve a cohesive finish.

CREATING THE BALANCE BETWEEN HOME & WORK

I get asked a lot about how I balance my home life with the business. Over the years, I haven't always got it right but I have learned some valuable things along the way. Our experiences will always be personal but these are the important lessons that have worked for our family.

In our constantly connected world, I believe it is vital to create a real discipline in our lives around 'time for home' and 'time for work'. Without this we cannot give either adequate attention. We need to be able to switch off and recharge properly.

I know when I am tired because I become ineffective, so it is vital for me to have a stop time every day, when I unplug from screens and my phone and leave any emails until the next morning. It is important to actively unwind (for me, that is usually a wonderful relaxing bath), to eat well, to make time for exercise and to sleep enough – those are the keys to feeling well and managing a busy life.

When I am working from home, I make sure to take breaks. I often stop halfway through the day and exercise, or walk the dogs outside. I then return to my desk refreshed and ready to go again.

As many of us now split our working hours between the office and home, a dedicated work area feels essential – somewhere we can work comfortably and effectively, that we can shut the door on or pack away at the end of the day.

No matter how small a space, it is worth making it special. Many of us spend most of the day working, so this space should also be uplifting and joyful. In my study at home, I love to have a lit scented candle, a few framed family photos, a pretty water jug and a vase with simple flowers or foliage. I usually have the dogs beside me as well, asleep on a very nice sofa!

All the home owners featured in this book have created beautiful spaces to work in too. Some display treasured pictures and beautiful paperweights, or the scissors and tools they like to use for their creative work. Others find clever ways for storage, such as lovely baskets hanging on hooks.

If you don't have a formal desk, use an occasional table in a space where you can concentrate well and where you feel inspired – close to a window is always a good idea. Make sure your table and a comfortable chair are at the right height and work out how you're going to file paperwork, to keep the space feeling calm, clear and organized.

I've learned that meticulous planning for the year ahead – especially important when our children were at school – is crucial. This has evolved as the children have grown, but for many years our 'life planning' has been run off a spreadsheet, with a column for each of us! Every important family date goes in first, including school and holidays, then we add in our work, travel and social commitments around them.

I'm fiercely protective of our weekends as a time for family. I try hard to get everyone to disconnect – phones really prevent us from enjoying the moment. It is so important to somehow carve out time and really enjoy the simple pleasures of life: going for a walk, cutting flowers from the garden, riding, reading, watching a match, cooking together – simply enjoying good times in each other's company.

I read a great article that said STOP trying to achieve a perfect work/life balance, as it does not exist. Every year, just before New Year, we actively re-evaluate our priorities for the 12 months ahead. It is never possible to do everything we would like to, but, as my husband always says, it is better to do five things really well than twenty badly.

I have learned not to be hard on myself and have accepted that not everything can be perfect. Perspective, kindness and good humour are much more important. Work happens every day, so it has to add value to family life, not diminish the joy.

ENTERTAINING &
KEEPING THINGS SIMPLE

I love nothing more than having people at home – sitting down for lunch or supper with
friends and family is one of life's real pleasures. They are moments to savour, take time over
and really enjoy, but with the busy lives we all lead today, I have also learned that keeping
things simple – and cheating well, when needed – are essential!

Find favourite dishes that work for you and your family, ones that can be easily scaled up and, ideally, prepared in advance. They don't always have to be homemade or complicated – remember, it is so much better to gather together around a lovely table than to spend too much time stuck in the kitchen.

We often choose to serve easy dishes that feed larger numbers of people well. Good, simple food, matched with beautiful presentation: a whole cooked salmon or ham on a stylish platter; a giant fish pie in a wonderful artisanal dish; charcuterie and cheese on a lazy Susan board; or a simple seasonal salad in a tactile wooden bowl. The way we dress our food can really elevate simple ingredients into something more special.

Make local farm shops and delis your best friends. I no longer feel guilty serving their delicious dishes when times are hectic. We often buy tray-baked brownies and mince pies but then present them beautifully, sprinkled in clouds of icing sugar. A couple of really good pieces of cheese, celery and special crackers are always popular too.

I rarely serve three courses now. Instead I love to have a few nibbles and plenty of drinks, and then offer just a main course with a pudding or cheese when we sit down. For pre-drink nibbles, my easy, go-to choices include quail's eggs with celery salt, an avocado dip (or bought dips) with seasonal, crunchy crudités and some artisan crisps in a pretty bowl.

For drinks, beautiful glasses make such a difference, and a great cocktail always gets a party going. It is a good idea to set up a small bar area with everything all ready, ice included. Drinks are so easy to dress up: a simple sprig of rosemary or mint, with a fresh slice of lemon or orange, makes even the humblest soft drink feel special. A strawberry in a glass of bubbles, an olive in a martini or a cinnamon stick in a warming glass of mulled wine all work beautifully too.

Laying a beautiful table is something that gives me so much pleasure. Over the years I have collected quite a few different types of china, glassware and linens, and now have several combinations that work really well together. Each one creates a slightly different feel and it is fun to keep mixing things up for a new look.

For a cosy midweek supper or relaxed lunch, artisanal plates and simple weighty cutlery and glassware work well. For a more glamorous dinner, a crisp white tablecloth, ribbon-tied napkins and fine, elegant glassware combine beautifully.

Napkins and placemats make a big difference too. They are brilliant for making the table look polished, whether it's bare or covered with a cloth. During the warmer months, I choose combinations that feel fresh and breezy, like seagrass and crisp cottons, while in winter I go for something with more texture.

Everyone looks great in candlelight, even at lunchtime! At night, candles create a magical atmosphere and I love to layer enough down the centre of the table, so that we can turn the main lights right down or off.

Seasonal flowers are an everyday joy. I always opt for simple and loose, never over-arranged and formal. One sprig can sometimes be all we need. I also love to use just greenery, herbs and grasses, mixed together for a fresh, natural look.

Depending on whether we are eating inside or out, we have cushions, blankets and shade ready in advance. A cosy throw over the back of a chair or a comfy cushion on a hard bench is always a welcome gesture, and in summer having sunshades already set up is a must.

Music sets the mood the moment our guests walk through the door, so having a few playlists ready is a great idea. I have several, covering everything from cocktails and relaxed summer days to Christmas jazz and a full-on family boogie!

Contributors

Industrial Edge
See pages 10–39

LUCILLE & RICHARD LEWIN

Lucille has enjoyed an illustrious career, founding retail brand Whistles in 1976 with her husband Richard. After the sale of Whistles in 2001, the couple established Chiltern Street Studio, a wholesale fashion business. Lucille worked as Creative Director at Liberty before returning to her roots in fine art, graduating with a Master's in Ceramics and Glass from The Royal College of Art. Exhibitions of her work have been curated at the V&A, Christie's and Connolly, London, and compelling pieces are layered throughout their London home.

lucillelewin.com
@lucillelewin

Inside–Outside
See pages 40–63

BARBARA WEISS

Born and raised in Italy, Barbara qualified as an architect in London, working subsequently for several years in prestigious design practices in both NYC and the UK. In 1987, she founded Barbara Weiss Architects, a medium-size practice known for bespoke, contextual projects and exacting design standards.
With a wide variety of architectural projects to her name, the majority of Barbara's commissions are residential. The extension to her family's Wiltshire home is a proud compendium of more than 30 years' experience.

barbaraweissarchitects.com
@barbaraweissarchitects

Heart & Soul
See pages 68–97

DR TIM EVANS

Dr Tim Evans (LVO) qualified in 1979 from the Westminster Hospital Medical School, and later spent time in Zimbabwe as the District Medical Officer on Lake Kariba. In 2000, Tim established the first fully integrated private General Practice at Westover House, London, incorporating the best in conventional, complementary and alternative health care. He was appointed in 2003 to the position of Apothecary to HM the Queen and The Royal Households of London. Tim built his Hampshire home with his late wife Annabel, and enjoys the space with his two children.

drtimevans.co.uk

Sartorial Elegance
See pages 98–115

Slow Architecture
See pages 120–135

Coastal Calm
See pages 136–161

**ANNA VALENTINE &
JONATHAN BERGER**

Anna's creative journey as a couture designer began in 1986. The vision for her Marylebone atelier has always been to create understated, exquisitely made, flattering clothing that makes every client feel and look their best. Anna works with her talented in-house team of designers, pattern-cutters, fitters and seamstresses, as well as artisanal specialists, to create highly personalized, bespoke finishes. Anna's home in Marylebone, London, exudes the same timeless style – a space that she shares with her husband Jonathan Berger, who works in the film and TV industry.

annavalentine.com
@annavalentine15

**SPENCER FUNG & TERESA
ROVIRAS**

Spencer was born in Hong Kong and came to England to study architecture at Cambridge and at the Architectural Association in London. He now works as a respected architect for many leading businesses, which are drawn to his sustainable design ethos. Catalonian-born Teresa has carved out a successful career as a design and creative consultant, and is the founder of online store Hedgehog. The couple share a passionate love of nature, which informs the style and design of their north London home where they live with their two children.

spencerfung.co.uk teresaroviras.co.uk
@spencer.fung @teresa.roviras

MARION LICHTIG

Marion trained in fashion and textiles at Central Saint Martins in London before moving into interiors. For the past 30 years, she has built a reputation for working in harmony with her clients, who are attracted to her trademark style. She favours simple, relaxed interiors that combine effortless, pared-back symmetry with antiques, and is known for sourcing covetable finds for her projects. Marion lives in London and completed this home in Cornwall on behalf of long-term clients.

marionlichtig.com
@marionlichtig
ckrock.com
@ck.living

Contributors

Artistic Licence
See pages 162–175

ELSA MIA ELPHICK & DAVID COOPER

Elsa and David met at Alexander McQueen in the early 2000s, when David was Menswear Creative Director, and Elsa a fashion designer. Now married, they live together in a rural Suffolk barn and share an under-the-radar passion for fashion and art. Elsa currently works as Head Designer for a contemporary womenswear brand, and David has returned to his fine art roots as a performance artist, sculptor and filmmaker. He was one of only ten international names awarded The Gilbert Bayes Award in 2021 by The Royal Society of Sculptors.

@elsamiaelphick
@headshaveholeshaveheads

Old Meets New
See pages 180–195

KAREN & ANTHONY CULL

Karen and Anthony, renowned for their understated and elegant eye, have carved out a successful business specializing in 18th-, 19th- and 20th-century Swedish, French and Belgian antiques, along with unique decorative finds and abstract art. A trusted source for private buyers, interior designers and trade antique dealers, they ship all over the world. The couple live in the rural Cotswolds and have created this new bolthole in Cheltenham as a more urban escape, combining the best of old and new in their trademark style.

antonandk.co.uk
@antonandkantiques

Lakeside House
See pages 212–231

JANE CLARK & MARK COPPING

Jane and Mark have both enjoyed illustrious careers, running their own respective head-hunting and design businesses. At the end of 2021, they bravely decided to step back from the corporate world in order to live more sustainably and follow their passion for mindful property renovation, and chose to sell their Rutland home. Their new business involves the environmentally aware transformation from the ground up of smaller-footprint homes, including a tired Grade II listed cottage in Rutland and the build of a sustainable, self-sufficient home on an old, established Portuguese estate.

janeandmark.co
@jane_and_mark

Creative Director

MARK WINSTANLEY

Chief Creative Officer of The White Company, Mark has worked collaboratively with founder Chrissie Rucker for over 15 years, building and growing the brand's presence across many important areas. Today, his responsibilities cover all creative aspects of the business, including digital, brochures and the visual presentation of the stores, as well as the strategic direction, design and buying of the Home collections. Mark's passion for design transcends the business, and carries through to the decoration of his own home. A passionate collector of both antiques and art, he lives with his family in East Sussex and Norfolk.

thewhitecompany.com

Contributing Editor & Creative Consultant

ALI HEATH

Ali is a writer, stylist, creative consultant and author, and has over 17 years' freelance experience, specializing in interiors and lifestyle. Her first book, *Curate,* was published in 2021, and her work is featured regularly in many prestigious titles, including *Country Living*, *Elle Decoration*, *Elle Decoration Country*, *Homes & Gardens*, *House & Garden*, *Livingetc*, *Modern Rustic*, *Red*, *Telegraph*, *The Times* and *You Magazine*. She collaborates with various leading photographers and her work is also syndicated internationally. Prior to going freelance, Ali set up a successful antiques business after working as New Business Director for a top, below-the-line marketing agency. She lives with her family in Surrey.

aliheath.co.uk
@aliheath_uk

Photographer

CHRIS EVERARD

Chris shot all of the photographs featured in this book on location in the UK during 2021. He relished the opportunity to shoot this second book for Chrissie Rucker, having photographed her first book *For the Love of White* in 2018. Chris shoots for many of the leading international interiors brands and magazines, and much of his work revolves around interior design and lifestyle. Chris studied fine art before moving into photography and has a long list of commercial clients to his name, including The White Company, Liberty, Zoffany and Drummonds. Although he specializes in interiors, his portfolio also includes portraiture, still lifes and landscapes. He lives with his family in London and Norfolk.

chris-everard.com
@chriseverard

Stylist

ELKIE BROWN

Elkie works in both the UK and the US as a stylist and art director specializing in interiors. She began her career as a merchandiser and buyer before moving into styling, and her work has been featured in numerous magazines, newspapers and books. Elkie works closely with many leading photographers and creative directors, while her commercial client list includes companies such as The White Company and Williams Sonoma, among many others. Her Pinterest account has more than 600,000 followers. She lives in London with her partner.

elkiebrown.com
@elkiestylist

Sourcebook

Aero Studios
200 Lexington Avenue,
Suite 1500, New York, NY 10016
aerostudios.com
@aerostudios

Anton & K
antonandk.co.uk
@antonandkantiques

Ardingly Antiques Fair
South of England Showground,
Ardingly, Nr Haywards Heath,
West Sussex RH17 6TL
iacf.co.uk/ardingly
@ardingly.antiques

AU
annaunwin.com
@anna.unwin

Brenda Antin
2400 South Grand Avenue,
Los Angeles, CA 90007
brendaantin.com
@brenda_antin

Claire Langley Antiques
The Warehouse,
Hallidays Yard, Radcliffe Road,
Stamford, Lincolnshire PE9 1ED
clairelangleyantiques.co.uk
@clairelangleyantiques

The Decorative Antiques and
Textiles Fair
Evolution London,
Battersea Park,
London SW11 4NJ
decorativefair.com
@decorativefair

Dix-Sept Antiques
17 Station Road, Woodbridge,
Suffolk IP13 9EA
@dixseptantiques

Drummonds
642 Kings Road,
London SW6 2DU
drummonds-uk.com
@Drummonds_uk

Farrow & Ball
farrow-ball.com
@farrowandball

Flow Gallery
1–5 Needham Road,
London W11 2RP
flowgallery.co.uk
@flowgallery

Foster & Gane
Three Pigeons, London Road,
Milton Common,
Thame, Oxfordshire OX9 2JN
fosterandgane.com
@fosterandgane

Francis Gallery
3 Fountain Buildings,
Lansdown Road,
Bath, Somerset BA1 5DU
francisgallery.co
@francisgallery

Freight
196 High Street, Lewes,
East Sussex BN7 2NS
freightstore.co.uk
@freighthhg

Galerie Half
6911 Melrose Avenue,
Los Angeles, CA 90038
galeriehalf.com
@galerie_half

Gallery BR
33 Long Street, Tetbury,
Gloucestershire GL8 8AA
gallerybr.co.uk
@gallery_br_

Giovanna Ticciati
New Street, Petworth,
West Sussex GU28 0AS
giovannaticciati.com
@giovannaticciati

Hedgehog
hedgehogshop.co.uk
@hedgehogshop

Hilary Batstone Antiques
84 Bourne Street,
London SW1W 8HQ
hilarybatstone.com
@hilarybatstone

HomeStories
homestories.com
@homestoriesnyc

HOWE London
93 Pimlico Road,
London SW1W 8PH
howelondon.com
@howelondon

John Derian Company
johnderian.com
@johnderiancompany

Josephine Ryan Antiques
44 Long Street, Tetbury,
Gloucestershire GL8 8AQ
josephineryanantiques.co.uk
@jryanantiques

Joshua Lumley
Stone Barn, Egerton,
Kent TN27 9AN
joshualumley.com
@joshualumleyantiquerugs

Labour and Wait
labourandwait.co.uk
@labourandwait

LASSCO Three Pigeons
London Road, Milton Common,
Oxfordshire OX9 2JN
lassco.co.uk
@lassco3pigeons

Lucille Lewin
lucillelewin.com
@lucillelewin

Maison Artefact
273 Lillie Road, London SW6 7LL
maisonartefact.com
@maisonartefact

MARCH
3075 Sacramento Street,
San Francisco, CA 94115
marchsf.com
@march.sf

Marchand Antiques
The Lodge, Grange Road, Platt,
Sevenoaks, Kent TN15 8LE
marchandantiques.co.uk
@marchand_antiques

Matthew Cox
19 St George's Square, Stamford,
Lincolnshire PE9 2BN
matthewcox.com
@matthewcoxetc

Maud and Mabel
10 Perrin's Court,
London NW3 1QS
maudandmabel.com
@maudandmabellondon

Monc XIII
40 Madison Street, Sag Harbor,
NY 11963
monc13.com
@moncxiii

Nām
22c New Bond Street, Bath,
Somerset BA1 1BA
namstore.co.uk
@namstore_bath

The New Craftsmen
34 North Row,
London W1K 6DG
thenewcraftsmen.com
@thenewcraftsmen

Nimmo and Spooner
277 Lillie Road, London SW6 7LL
nimmoandspooner.co.uk
@nimmoandspooner

Obsolete
11270 Washington Boulevard,
Culver City, CA 90230
obsoleteinc.com
@obsoleteinc

Papers and Paints
4 Park Walk, London SW10 0AD
papersandpaints.co.uk
@papersandpaints

Paula Rubenstein NY
195 Chrystie Street, New York,
NY 10002
paularubenstein.com
@paularubenstein

Plain English Design
plainenglishdesign.co.uk
@plainenglishkitchens

Plain Goods
17 East Shore Road,
New Preston, CT 06777
plain-goods.com
@plaingoodsshop

Puckhaber Decorative Antiques
281 Lillie Road, London SW6 7LL
1 High Street, Rye, East Sussex
TN31 7JE
puckhaberdecorativeantiques.
com
@puckhaberdecor

Robert Young Antiques
68 Battersea Bridge Road,
London SW11 3AG
robertyoungantiques.com
@robertyoungantiques

Roman and Williams Guild
53 Howard Street, New York,
NY 10010
rwguild.com
@rwguild

Rose Uniacke
76–84 Pimlico Road,
London SW1W 8PL
roseuniacke.com
@roseuniacke

Societique
Green Street Chapel,
Morecambe,
Lancashire LA4 5HN
societique.co.uk
@societique

Spencer Fung
spencerfung.co.uk
@spencer.fung

Sunbury Antiques Market
Kempton Park Racecourse,
Staines Road East, Sunbury-on-
Thames, Surrey TW16 5AQ
Sandown Park Racecourse,
Portsmouth Road, Esher,
Surrey KT10 9AJ
sunburyantiques.com
@sunburyantiques

Wilson Stephens & Jones Gallery
71 Westbourne Park Road,
London W2 5QH
16 High Street, Bruton,
Somerset BA10 0AA
wsjgallery.com
@wsjgallery_london

The White Company Stores

UK

ABERDEEN
Union Square Mall, Guild Square, Aberdeen
AB11 5RG

BATH
15 Northgate Street, Bath, Avon BA1 5AS

BEVERLEY
Unit A, 44 Toll Gavel, 2 Cross Street, Beverley
HU17 9AX

BICESTER
2 Pingle Drive, Bicester Village, Oxfordshire
OX26 6WD

BIRMINGHAM GRAND CENTRAL
Unit 2B, Stephenson Place, Birmingham B2 4BF

BLUEWATER
Unit L103, Bluewater Shopping Centre, Lower
Guildhall, Greenhithe, Kent DA9 9ST

BRENT CROSS
Upper Ground Level Metropolitan Mall, Brent
Cross Shopping Centre, London NW4 3FP

BRIGHTON
4 North Street, Brighton BN1 1EB

BRISTOL
Unit 134/135 Upper Level, The Mall at Cribbs
Causeway, Bristol BS34 5DG

BROMLEY
Unit 236-227, Upper Shopping Mall, The Glades
Shopping Centre, Bromley BR1 1DN

CAMBRIDGE
SU 53, Upper Mall, Grand Arcade, Cambridge
CB2 3BJ

CAMP HOPSON
7-11 Northbrook Street, Newbury RG14 1DN

CANARY WHARF
Unit 70, Jubilee Place, Canary Wharf, London
E14 5NY

CARDIFF
Unit LG, 22-23 & 24, St David's Mall, Cardiff
CF10 2DP

CHELMSFORD
Bond Street, Chelmsford CM1 1GH

CHELTENHAM
84 The Promenade, Cheltenham GL50 1NB

CHESTER
19 Northgate Street, Chester CH1 2HA

CHICHESTER
73 North Street, Chichester PO19 1LB

COVENT GARDEN
Unit 5, Slingsby Place, St Martin's Courtyard,
London WC2E 9AB

EDINBURGH
88 George Street, Edinburgh EH2 3BU

ELYS WIMBLEDON
16 George's Road, Wimbledon,
London SW19 4DP

EXETER
230 High Street, Exeter EX4 3NE

FENWICK CANTERBURY
St Georges Street, Canterbury CT1 2TB

FENWICK NEWCASTLE
Northumberland Street, Newcastle Upon Tyne
NE1 7DE

GLASGOW
123 Buchanan Street, Glasgow G1 2JA

GUILDFORD
Unit 6B, Tunsgate Quarter, Guildford GU1 3QY

HARRODS
87-135 Brompton Road, Knightsbridge, London
SW1X 7XL

HARROGATE
8 James Street, Harrogate HG1 1RF

HOOPERS WILMSLOW
35 Alderley Road, Wilmslow SK9 1PB

KINGSTON
14-16 Market Place,
Kingston Upon Thames, KT1 1JP

KINGSTON BENTALLS
Wood Street, Kingston Upon Thames, KT1 1TX

LEEDS
Unit 4 Victoria Gate, Harewood Street, Leeds
LS2 7AR

LIVERPOOL ONE
9 Peter's Lane, Liverpool L1 3DE

MANCHESTER
21-23 King Street, Manchester M2 6AF

MARKET HARBOROUGH
10 High Street, Market Harborough LE16 7NJ

MARLOW
30-32 High Street, Marlow SL7 1AW

MARYLEBONE HIGH STREET
112-114 Marylebone High Street,
London W1U 4SA

MEADOWHALL
24 Park Lane, Meadowhall, Sheffield S9 1EL

MILTON KEYNES
32 Silbury Arcade, The Centre: MK, Milton Keynes MK9 3AG

NEWCASTLE
Unit SU5, Monument Mall, Newcastle Upon Tyne NE1 7AL

NORWICH
22-23 Gentleman's Walk, Norwich NR2 1NA

NOTTINGHAM
15 St Peter's Gate, Nottingham NG1 2JF

OXFORD
7/8 Queen Street, Oxford OX1 1EJ

PORTSMOUTH
Unit 60, Gunwharf Quays, Portsmouth PO1 3TZ

SELFRIDGES BIRMINGHAM
Upper Mall East, Bullring, Birmingham B5 4BP

SELFRIDGES LONDON
400 Oxford Street, London W1A 1AB

SELFRIDGES TRAFFORD
1 The Dome, The Trafford Centre, Manchester M17 8DA

SOLIHULL
Mall Square Shopping Centre, 2 Mill Lane, Solihull B91 3AX

ST. ALBANS
5 Christopher Place Shopping Centre, St. Albans AL3 5DQ

ST. PANCRAS
Arcade Unit 9, St Pancras Station, London N1C 4QP

STAMFORD
19 High Street, Stamford PE9 2AL

STRATFORD UPON AVON
23 Bridge Street, Stratford Upon Avon CV37 6AD

SOUTHAMPTON
Unit SU20, West Quay Shopping Centre, Southampton SO15 1QE

SYMONS STREET
4 Symons Street, London SW3 2TJ

TRURO
14/15 Boscawan Street, Truro TR1 2QU

TUNBRIDGE WELLS
28-30 High Street, Tunbridge Wells TN1 1XB

VOISINS
PO Box 9, 26-32 King Street, St Helier, Jersey JE4 8NF

WESTFIELD LONDON
SU1207, Ariel Way, Westfield London, London W12 7HT

WESTFIELD STRATFORD CITY
157 The Street, Westfield Stratford City, Montifichet Road, Olympic Park, London E20 1EN

WINCHESTER
30 High Street, Winchester SO23 9BL

WINDSOR
18-19 King Edward Court, Windsor SL4 1TF

YORK
26-28 Stonegate, York YO1 8AS

DUBLIN
72 Grafton Street, Dublin, Ireland DO2 Y757

KILDARE
Unit 65, Kildare Village, Nurney Road, County Kildare, Ireland R51 R265

www.thewhitecompany.com

US

www.nordstrom.com/brands/the-white-company--19437

For online orders in the UK, Europe and North America visit www.thewhitecompany.com

Index

— Page numbers in *italics* refer to photographs —

Author's Acknowledgements

After the very generous response to our first book, *For the Love of White*, it has been such an inspiring process and pleasure to create *The Art of Living with White* as the next in the series. It has been an extremely thoughtful and collaborative journey because we particularly wanted to find and showcase very different homes from those we featured before.

I am immensely grateful to all the homeowners who have allowed us the privilege of sharing their homes and for the time they have given to share their stories and their personal ways of living with white. You have given us so many new and inspiring ideas to draw from.

To my incredible team at The White Company, you are the reason this is such a special business – and I would particularly like to thank Mark Winstanley, David MacLeary, Sophie Powell and Caroline Hollinrake because without you this book would not have become a reality.

To my publisher Alison Starling and to the extended team from Octopus Publishing – Jonathan Christie, Sybella Stephens, Helen Ridge and Katherine Hockley – thank you all so much for your belief in our second book together.

To Ali Heath, my contributing editor and creative consultant, thank you for our enjoyable interviews, your intuitive insights into the worlds of each homeowner, and your wonderful energy and commitment. To photographer Chris Everard – as ever, every single one of your images comes with such perfectionism – and to interior stylist Elkie Brown, my biggest thanks for your impeccable styling.

To my late mum Rosie – you are missed more than words can express, but your legacy of love, family and the importance of home remains at the heart of all I do. To my dad Anthony, my stepfather Simon and stepmother Jane, thank you for your unconditional love and support. And to Granny Rucker and Uncle Esmond – who left me the shares that I sold to start this business – I never forget you are the reason I have been able to do this.

To my husband Nick and our children, Tom, Ella, Indie and Bea – you are all my world and what makes our home such a special place to be.

There is so much love in this book – I am beyond grateful to you all.

Chrissie x

First published in Great Britain in 2022 by Mitchell Beazley,
an imprint of Octopus Publishing Group Ltd.

HarperCollins books may be purchased for educational, business,
or sales promotional use. For information please email the
Special Markets Department at SPsales@harpercollins.com.

Published in 2022 by
Harper Design
An Imprint of HarperCollins*Publishers*
195 Broadway
New York, NY 10007
Tel: (212) 207-7000
Fax: (855) 746-6023
harperdesign@harpercollins.com
www.hc.com

Distributed in North America by
HarperCollins Publishers
195 Broadway
New York, NY 10007

ISBN 978-0-06-323055-2

Library of Congress Control Number: 2022933302

Printed and bound in China

22 23 24 25 26 10 9 8 7 6 5 4 3 2 1

FSC
www.fsc.org

MIX
Paper from
responsible sources
FSC® C008047

Contributing Editor and Creative Consultant: Ali Heath
Photographer: Chris Everard
Photographic Stylist: Elkie Brown
Publisher: Alison Starling
Creative Director: Jonathan Christie
Senior Managing Editor: Sybella Stephens
Copy Editor: Helen Ridge
Senior Production Manager: Katherine Hockley
For The White Company:
Chief Creative Officer: Mark Winstanley
Head of Creative Operations: David MacLeary
Shoot Producer: Sophie Powell